CHRONICLE
OF A CRISIS
FORETOLD

W0087062

PAUL SCHREYER

Chronicle of a Crisis Foretold

How a Virus Could Change the World

OVALmedia

This work, including all its parts, is protected by copyright.
No part of this book may be reproduced, distributed, or transmitted,
in any form or by any means, including reproduction, translation, microfilming,
or storage and processing using electronic or mechanical methods,
without the prior written consent of the publisher, except
in the case of brief quotations embodied in reviews and certain
other non-commercial uses permitted by copyright law.

ISBN 978-3-949559-03-7
© Westend Verlag, Frankfurt/Main, 2020
© Oval Media, 2021, Christburger Straße 47, D-10405 Berlin
For more information on this topic, please visit our website:
https://www.oval.media

Supplementary material for the book can be found
by scanning the QR code below or via the following link:

https://www.oval.media/bonus-materials

Design: Buchgut, Berlin
Print: Friedrich Pustet GmbH & Co. KG, Regensburg
Printed in Germany

Translation by
Susan R. Berger

Preface to the English Edition

The original German edition of this book was one of the most read books in Germany in the autumn and winter of 2020.[1] The video of a lecture based on this book was viewed on the Internet by more than two million people.[2] In other words, this book was being talked about in Germany, but—and this qualification is important—not in the mainstream media, which totally ignored it and placed an almost complete blackout on the book and the facts and ideas it presents. Because, in these times, information spreads, even when the classical media attempts to conceal it, this kind of suppression—as has become the case with many critical books recently—no longer always works. This, I believe, is one of the small signs of hope in the current crisis.

I wrote this book between April and July 2020, at the beginning of the coronavirus crisis. One might therefore think that much of the material would now be outdated. But, as reading this book more than a year later shows, this is not the case. The two focal points in this book—an insight into the more than twenty-year history preceding the current events and a chronicle of the first three months of the crisis—continue to provide helpful material for understanding the developments since then. Nevertheless, time goes on and new knowledge emerges. For this translation, I have added a chapter dealing with a serious but barely noticed quake in the financial markets that occurred three months before the outbreak of the coronavirus crisis. I only discovered this fact after the work on the original manuscript had already been completed. I think it is essential.

Paul Schreyer, April 2021

Introduction

To begin with, I would like to ask a question of you, the reader of this book: Do you believe you understand the coronavirus crisis? Do you feel you have fully grasped and understood what has been happening in the world since January 2020? When I began working on this book in April 2020, I hadn't. And even now, three months later, although I have accumulated more background information and additional hypotheses, I have not yet found the one big, irrefutable explanation that many people understandably want.

I would like to encourage all readers to consider this uncertainty as something positive. Premature certainty leads to tunnel vision and to blocking out or rejecting anything that doesn't fit the picture that has already been formed. The current events have many aspects and protagonists—too many in my view—to be able to hope for complete clarity over a short time, and six months is very short for this kind of world event. Nevertheless, collecting information from a wide range of sources, weighing and classifying it, and recognizing the gaps and ambiguities that remain—all this is possible and also necessary. And this is exactly where this book can help.

COVID-19 is a very dangerous disease for many people and has led to great suffering. In this book, none of this is intended to be trivialized or played down. However, some of the "certainties" surrounding the virus and the pandemic that are being publicly disseminated often do not stand up to closer scrutiny (see Chapters 8 to 10). The ambiguities begin with the contentious conditions for declaring a pandemic.[3] When does a viral respiratory disease officially become a global disaster? A publication by the World Health Organization (WHO) acknowledges that the declaration of a pandemic[4] "depends on a host of arbitrary factors."[5] As the research makes clear, it is not only about pure science, but also always about politics.

Considerable space on the following pages is given to the history behind the crisis, in particular the section dealing with pandemic and emergency plans as they were implemented in 2020. For me, personally, it was surprising to discover during the research how intensely and for how long such viral outbreaks have been rehearsed, time and again, especially in the US, and how regularly a political state of emergency, including public unrest and the restriction of civil rights, has been played out in this context.

In addition to these plans, simulation exercises, and political entanglements, there has also, for some time, been a noticeably worrying development in medicine and the natural sciences. In my opinion, this is essential background to the current crisis. This book will therefore begin with some more fundamental observations on this.

Paul Schreyer, July 2020

Prologue:
False Guiding Lights

On a mild spring evening in April 2020, during the period when contact with others was prohibited and shortly before the start of mandatory mask-wearing, my wife and I stood in the garden watering the vegetable patch. We had arrived home late and the sun had long since set, so I illuminated the delicate plants with a flashlight while my wife waved the watering can over them. Besides the soft sound of the sprinkling water and a distant bird call, there was complete silence. Peace was in the air.

When we were finished, we looked up to the starry sky for a moment. My wife noticed it first: "Look, something is moving." In fact, a small point of light was moving slowly across the sky; since it wasn't flashing, it was apparently not an airplane. Perhaps it was a satellite? But that too seemed unlikely because we then saw another point of light appear, following the first. A third point appeared, then a fourth, a fifth—all spaced at the same distance apart and going in the same direction with the same speed on the same path. Several dozen evenly moving "stars" moved across the deep dark sky like a string of pearls.

The silent spectacle lasted almost half an hour. Fascinated, we stared upwards. Had we just witnessed a column of passing UFOs? We watched and followed attentively, looking at the train of lights without being able to make rhyme or reason of it—a strange sensation.

Back in the house, we did what one does these days: We searched the Internet. Disillusionment quickly followed. These were no UFOs, no puzzles, no mystery—instead, we had merely been seeing a part of the American billionaire Elon Musk's huge satellite fleet, Starlink, move across the night sky.

Musk, the chief executive of electric carmaker Tesla, we discovered, employs a large portion of his fortune on aerospace plans, in particular the production of rockets that are capable of carrying loads into space. One of his goals is to colonize Mars. In his view, the next evolutionary step is to make human life "multi-planetary."[6] In May 2019, as part of another project, he began shooting satellites into the earth's orbit to provide global broadband Internet coverage through his company SpaceX. According to Musk, satellites anywhere in the world should "meet the growth in users' anticipated needs."[7] This was a market worth billions. In the early stages of its plans, Google had already secured a stake in SpaceX with a large investment.[8] Musk planned to produce a total of 40,000 (!) satellites to orbit the earth, 400 of which were already in space in the spring of 2020. We had just seen some of these.

On reading about this, my initial astonishment mixed with anger. What was this man claiming for himself, cluttering the eternally silent star-studded sky with modern high-tech that would subsequently become useless electronic waste in the not-too-distant future? Astronomers were already warning that their science was in serious jeopardy from the billionaire's plans, as these countless moving points of light could make the observation of celestial bodies and distant galaxies impossible.[9]

But Musk, closely affiliated with the US administration, on whose behalf he also sends secret espionage satellites into space,[10] apparently stopped at nothing. The world itself, covered with a network of tens of thousands of flying devices, became his toy. His plans appeared excessive and disturbing. Their implementation, however, was carried out quietly and generally without resistance.

Why, one might ask, does a book about the coronavirus crisis begin, of all things, with Elon Musk and his space plans? What does the virus, the worldwide political state of emergency, and the debate about fundamental rights and vaccines have to do with the private satellite program of a billionaire?

At first glance, very little. Nevertheless, it seems that both developments reflect a deeper trend. Corporate governance measures and technologies are becoming increasingly and effectively coordinated on a worldwide and central scale. Influential private individuals are creating strategies for the entire world that are increasingly also being implemented globally.[11] The solution often lies in processes that are lifeless, automated, and far from human, and which, although they promise convenience, also enable central domination and control—as well as extraordinary profits. At the end of this development there is great unification. Special technologies and programs driven by a few oligarchs become binding for everyone—without any democratic debate.

The problem extends far beyond the current crisis. A kind of autopilot seems to be controlling a great deal, whether in politics, the economy or even in general thinking. Responsibility for decisions is becoming increasingly lost in the fog of international organizations or is immediately transferred to algorithms and thus detached from individual or personal considerations.

The popular assumption that some superrich individuals could become the new world rulers is obvious, but it does not adequately explain the situation. It seems that these influential people are also blinded by an ideology that is taking on a life of its own. It is as if the process of reflection itself—individual assessment, doubt, and questioning—is being increasingly extinguished to give way to a trust in automated efficiency.

Human beings, who by their nature are free, self-determining and living beings, are experiencing a degradation and devaluation in the course of this trend. They are becoming interchangeable objects, intensely scrutinized "data points" in an information network that is beyond their control. People will always fit best into this system, which is currently being perfected, when they themselves act as predictably and efficiently as machines.

The Russian philosopher Nikolai Berdyaev had already referred to the consequences of the triumph of technology in the 1940s, long before today's computer age:

> "The power of technology has very difficult consequences for a person whose soul is not sufficiently adapted. There is a tremendous acceleration of time, a speed that man cannot catch up with. Incredible activity is required of a person that does not allow themselves to be themselves. But this activity makes a person passive. He becomes an instrument outside the human process, merely a function of the production process. The activity of the human spirit is weakened. Man is assessed as utilitarian, according to his productivity. This is an alienation of human nature and the destruction of humanity."[12]

Wherever one looks, regardless of profession or industry, everything and everyone must work as quickly and efficiently as possible and integrate themselves into a precisely prefabricated pattern—like a robot with no will of its own. It is all about functioning. The question of for whom and why is not even taken into consideration.

The author Hauke Ritz sees this development as a breach of civilization—for the first time in centuries, man is no longer seen as a free and individually unique being:

"Ultimately, both the Christian Middle Ages and the humanist modern society are linked by considering each person to be unique. As a result, human beings are given responsibility and criminal liability. This image of humans has been increasingly interpreted politically in modern times and has thus became the basis of all the political and social utopias that have shaped Europe—from the French Revolution to the end of the Cold War. ... Today's algorithm-controlled data monitoring, on the other hand, is based on a completely different image of humans and a completely different relationship to their history, i.e., one that sees individual human beings only as generic specimens whose purchasing behavior, preferences, and even mental development can, in principle, be predicted by comparing them with millions of others. ... Under these conditions, human freedom, in the sense it has been understood until now, is basically no longer possible."[13]

And it is not only freedom that is dwindling, but also, as a peculiar ramification, the intellect. The further technology advances, the more the free, independent spirit appears to be in retreat. Decisions that have been made, whether in politics, the economy, or in administration, seem more often to be dumb, insensitive, and shortsighted. Why is this so? Why have people allowed themselves to act like machines without personalities of their own, and why have they accepted being treated this way? What is this virus that has infected society?

Currently, the issue is vaccination. In April 2020, in the midst of the COVID-19 state of emergency, Microsoft founder, Bill Gates, one of the wealthiest men in the world, announced the following in an interview on the German broadcaster *ARD's* daily news magazine program, *Tagesthemen*:

> "And this is a vaccine we're going to give to seven billion people. ... And eventually, we'll scale this thing up so that everyone on this planet can get the vaccine."[14]

The first question one could ask about this unbelievable statement is who is "we"? Gates' legitimation exists in a vacuum. No one has elected him or, in any other way, democratically empowered him. All that he has to show for himself are the billions with which he supports the WHO and various other health-related organizations. He sees himself as an altruistic patron yet behaves as the (unelected) spokesman of a quasi-global government.

The second question to Gates' announcement is of the necessity, or even appropriateness, of the solution he has presented. One of the most astounding aspects of the coronavirus crisis is the speed with which the world's governments have agreed that a global vaccination campaign is the only reasonable response to the newly discovered virus. This conclusion is anything but compelling. Why, for example, was a global campaign to strengthen our immune systems not launched instead? After all, this virus, like many other pathogenic agents, is largely only deadly for persons with unusually weak immune systems: the very old, frail, sick, those who are badly undernourished, and those who are stressed. So, why in the world is a vaccine that will basically change nothing in the immune systems of the groups at risk being touted with such force—especially since a weak immune system is also the gateway for numerous other viruses and pathogens? Irrespective of this one individual virus, would it not be more appropriate to start exactly here, with, for example, a radical reduction in stress and work pressure, a public education program on healthy nutrition without the interference of lobby interests, and social programs to promote increased relaxation, well-being, and humanity. All these, added together, would significantly strengthen the immune systems of the public and massively reduce the numbers of deceased from the epidemic. So, why is a controversial, risky, and highly specialized technical solution, which ignores the fundamental problems, but through which a few businesses will earn a great deal of money, being put into effect rather than a more obvious, far-reaching solution?

This question touches on a sore point in modern medicine that has long been part of an industry that is less defined by empathy and humanity than by a ruthless struggle for market share.[15] It may be trivial, but it should always be remembered that diseases create markets for medications and treatment methods—the more expensive, the better, and the more patients, the more profit. A healthy society does not, by definition, lie in the interests of this industry.

This connection is one of the great taboos of our time. After all, if the private pharmaceutical, hospital, medical technology, and "health management" industries are wholly dependent on more and more people being sicker for longer to ensure their rising stock prices—which is exactly, objectively speaking, unfortunately the case—how can society allow this industry to remain in the hands of profit-oriented investors without causing lasting damage to itself? What is more, how can society imagine that this industry will be an honest "partner" in the prevention of diseases?

We live in a time of technological faith. All major problems should be technically solvable. Products and processes launched by corporations offer promises of happiness and salvation, like those that were previously reserved for religions. This development is not new, it has been taking place all over the world for more than a hundred years. Original human instincts and traditional experiences from past generations are worth little compared to technological innovations or anything that can somehow be machine-produced and clearly measured. One comes to rely more and more on "the numbers" and less and less on intuition, which is no longer trusted because it cannot be measured.

Among the chief engineers in Silicon Valley, around Google, Apple, and Microsoft, an ideology has spread that takes this way of thinking to frightening perfection. It is "the technicians who define how the world should be."[16] Anything that can be digitally ascertainable in some way is measured, evaluated, and transformed into algorithms. Artificial intelligence is considered a divine promise, striving for the technical perfection of human beings ("transhumanism"), with some business leaders even dreaming of immortality by "uploading" the human spirit to machine bodies.[17] This requires an interface on which work is already being vigorously done, including by Elon Musk, who founded his own company called Neuralink in 2016 for precisely this purpose. The media commented on this as follows:

"The vision is that, in the distant future, it will be possible to transmit skills, for example martial arts sequences or the learning of a new foreign language, via an app store chip in the brain. Neuralink wants to merge people with artificial intelligence (AI) in this way. Musk is afraid that AI will overwhelm humans. This could be prevented by combining humans with AI via the BCI (brain-computer interface)."[18]

The underlying motive for this research, so it seems, is also a fear of the "magic powers" that are being used. The author Philipp von Becker clarifies:

"Transhumanism stands in the tradition of the great utopias of the early modern era ... in which the future of human beings, in the spirit of the scientific belief in progress, was envisioned as a reclaimed paradise. In the further course of modern times, however, literary-philosophical utopias became dystopias [pessimistic images of the future] in which humans were no longer masters of nature but become enslaved to themselves through the miracle of technology and science."[19]

Besides excessive measuring and enhancing, a great desire for clarity has taken hold of many people. This also has a political dimension. In view of increasing insecurity and acute danger, from social disintegration to political extremism, and as far as deadly viruses, people increasingly look for stability in unshakeable truths and rigid prohibitions. The principles with which they want to arm themselves are rigidity, conflict, and intransigence. These are the methods of war.

Common beliefs include: Radically fight the populists! Eradicate the coronavirus! Ban conspiracy theories! The atmosphere is constantly tense, the truth is obvious, the enemy is clearly recognizable, and the world can be explained on a black-and-white grid: good versus evil, enlightened versus backward, responsible versus deluded. Anyone who disturbs this new, militant harmony is considered dangerous. The Islamic scholar Thomas Bauer describes the trend towards explicitness as a new fundamentalism:

"Those who seek unambiguity will insist that there can always be only one truth, and that this truth is also clearly recognizable. A perspective, and thus ambiguous, view of the world is rejected. ... Diversity, complexity and plurality are often no longer perceived as enrichment."[20]

The reason for this is easy to understand. In order to find ambiguity enriching, a somewhat relaxed and calm life in reasonably stable circumstances is necessary. Ambiguity and lack of clarity are intimidating. In order to deal with them, the kinds of reserves that fewer and fewer people have in today's constant stress are needed. Threatened by fear and danger, views become radicalized, perspectives narrow, and people become more easily manageable.

This line of thought is often used to explain why critical views of the elite have spread in recent years: People are overwhelmed by the complexity and multidimensional nature of the world and long for simple explanations and easy-to-understand stories of shadowy accomplices, traffickers, and evil powers. Less attention is paid to similar developments at the other end of society, but there the signs are reversed. Thus, many people believe (or hope) that those at the upper end of society—governments, media owners, intelligence agencies, the superrich—behave more or less arbitrarily, without a greater plan, or at least without a plan that would harm the majority. Secret agreements at the expense of the general public could "never" be kept secret and would therefore not exist, according to this conviction.[21] Both attitudes—the strict orientation towards "conspiracy theories" as well as their blanket denial—belong together structurally and are an expression of the same longing for clarity.

The desire for unambiguous truths has become particularly evident during the coronavirus crisis through the divergent differences of ideas. Scientists who view the virus and its dangers differently from the government and its advisers are generally referred to in many media outlets as cranks, attention-seekers, and conspiracy theorists.

The idea that science can only develop in a discourse between different perspectives seems to have almost disappeared. Instead, more and more people believe that "science" has proven either this or that—as if a group of experts who, by virtue of clearly-proven, undeniable arguments, are naturally all in agreement. Of course, undisputed scientific findings do exist. In many cases, however, the imputed consent of the researchers is only a facade promoted by interest groups, each of which gives authority to a very specific point of view. The supposed enlightenment of people who say they trust only "science" is often little more than a modern form of faith in authority.

The fact that truth in a society is never detached from power is rarely discussed. The media scientist Michael Meyen says: "The science that is only interested in truth and in nothing else is a political fairy tale, a mirage."[22] The influence of economic interests on the media and on science appears to be another taboo of our time.

This becomes particularly problematic when private interest groups, governments, and the media *in unison* declare certain views to be true and others to be absurd, i.e., when they combine their ability to publicly give authority to selected individuals, while at the same time marginalizing others. The message "Listen to Drosten, don't believe Wodarg!"[23] was consistent across the mainstream German media in the spring of 2020.

In this way, truth is "decreed," and fair debate is made impossible. At the same time, censorship flourishes—today no longer applied by the state as it previously was, but rather by the large Internet corporations. Whoever deviates from and threatens the credibility of the official narratives is increasingly removed from YouTube, Facebook, etc., and also, meanwhile, at the express request of doctors. This extract is taken from a letter published in May 2020 by a group of doctors, including the German government advisor, Prof Christian Drosten:

"The tidal wave of false and misleading content surrounding the coronavirus is not an isolated outbreak of disinformation, but part of a global problem. ... These lies are important because they ... want to dissuade people from getting vaccinated ... That is why we are calling on technology companies today to take immediate and systematic action to stop the flood of medical misinformation and the resulting health crisis."[24]

This international media appeal, which, among other things, was placed as a full-page advert in the *New York Times*, was a call for a comprehensive suppression of unwelcome information.

This trend of a standardization and "disambiguation" of the world, where everything and everyone is to be subordinated, is disturbing. The global focus on the coronavirus has made it possible to radically accelerate this development that has been observably gaining momentum for years. Behind the crisis, whose emergence and history can be traced on the following pages, a totalitarian utopia that runs counter to the principles of a free, peaceful, and diverse civilization, appears more and more clearly. It is the vision of a "perfect," centrally-controlled world in which individual freedom becomes a rare luxury.

The author Aldous Huxley, in his dark 1932 novel *Brave New World*, prefaced a gloomy future with a quote from the abovementioned philosopher Nikolai Berdyaev that is no less topical today:

"Utopias are feasible. Life is moving towards them. And perhaps a new era is beginning in which intellectuals and the educated class think about how utopias can be prevented and a non-utopian, less perfect and freer society returns."

The first step on this road is possibly a return to human coexistence without fear, distancing, and masks, but instead, with affection, trust and solidarity. As the American philosopher and author Charles Eisenstein put it in March 2020:

"There is an alternative to the paradise of perfect control that our civilization has so long pursued, and that recedes as fast as our progress, like a mirage on the horizon. Yes, we can proceed as before down the path toward greater insulation, isolation, domination, and separation. We can normalize heightened levels of separation and control, believe that they are necessary to keep us safe, and accept a world in which we are afraid to be near each other. Or we can take advantage of this pause, this break in normal, to turn onto a path of reunion, of holism, of the restoring of lost connections, of the repair of community and the rejoining of the web of life."[25]

This "web of life" is constantly being cut up into the thinnest threads by super-specialized scientific research and digital high-performance medication. Complex biological systems are broken down into isolated building blocks that are then arbitrarily modified and reassembled. The author Hauke Ritz describes the spirit behind this as follows:

"The essence of the natural sciences is based on the unspoken hypothesis that what is alive only appears to be alive because, due to its complexity, it cannot yet be fully understood. If and when science is in a position to fully comprehend this complexity of living, however, that which is alive would also be revealed as actually being dead. ... In view of this, it is not surprising that the natural sciences, as a whole, can explain the dead very well, whereas, to this day, they have difficulty in understanding the living. ...

"The sciences began as an unbiased thought process that questioned religious dogmas. However, the more the natural sciences committed themselves to understanding the world as a fundamentally dead, determined, subjectless, unfree and unconscious system of deprivation, the more they themselves began to put forward a new metaphysic [an unprovable philosophy] that has finally assumed a dogmatic form in the course of industrialization.

"Against this background, the question arises as to what extent this denial of freedom by today's natural sciences also influences the overall tendencies of technical progress. Can we draw conclusions about the direction and developmental logic in technological progress itself from the world view that underlies the natural sciences? ... Could a natural science that, in principle, denies human freedom end up producing a technology of the unfree world by necessity?"[26]

These are far-reaching ideas that may help us better understand the state of emergency triggered by the coronavirus crisis. For it is possible that what has turned politics and society upside down since the beginning of 2020 is not merely a single virus— but rather the crisis of an ideology.

Delusion and Reality:
Dealing with Conspiracy Theories

Many people experienced the first weeks and months of the coronavirus crisis in a confused, frightened state of shock. Some felt that they had been helplessly extradited into a nightmare which simply would not end.[27] Everything seemed unreal. How could it be that, in such a short time, the most basic rules of coexistence were revoked all over the world? And all of this merely because of a virus? Was that believable?

It is not surprising that, in a crisis, all sorts of different theories and attempts at explanation circulate and find millions of followers. Everyone tries in their own way to make sense of the impending chaos and the all-pervading fear: Is everything ultimately planned? Is Bill Gates behind it all? Why mass vaccinations? What is the contact tracing app all about? Is a global totalitarian order being established in which the tech companies assume full power? Has the US attacked its main competitor China with a bioweapon? Is China secretly fighting back? Is globalization going to be shut down in order to "pull the plug" on China? What is true anymore? And who can be believed? The government? Television? Or the "alternative media"?

In view of these questions and theories, public concern is growing over the fear of a new irrationality. Fear of the virus is accompanied by a dread of the spread of an enigmatic madness that captures minds and confuses, especially in the form of so-called conspiracy theories. "The world seems to have gone mad," says the author Andreas Wehr, describing how he perceives such theories:

"It is not the coronavirus that needs to be fought, but Bill Gates and his foundation. It is not the lack of a vaccine against the new disease COVID-19 that is the problem, but that vaccinations are the work of the devil. It is not the attacks on the WHO by Trump that are reprehensible, but the alleged collusion of this organization with Big Pharma. It is not the federal government's lax attitude towards the rising pandemic that is the scandal, but the restrictions on contact that it has imposed and with which it has taken its own population hostage. These and similar accusations are what participants in the Berlin 'hygiene demonstrations' are saying, along with the nichtohneuns.de [not without us] gatherings in Munich, or the demonstrations of the Initiative Querdenken [lateral thinkers] 711 in Stuttgart, as well as at protest marches and gatherings in many other parts of the country. ... Devout mystics, followers of brazen conspiracy fantasies, notorious anti-vaccination activists and history falsifiers ... dominate the field."[28]

The tone is rough, but the issue is far from new. Warnings about conspiracy theories have been around for a long time, but now, since the spring of 2020, they have a new volume and vehemence. Such views have clearly become a major threat. But for whom exactly? Only for reason and facts?

The term conspiracy theory has a distinct peculiarity that is rarely mentioned: It does not mean what it claims to mean. Whoever uses the expression only rarely really describes a theory about a conspiracy. That would be rather unspectacular. Conspiracies are part of everyday life, especially in the world of business, as seen, for example, in the diesel emissions scandal or in the secret price-fixing deals between companies that are occasionally uncovered by tenacious investigators and independent courts of law.[29] Nor are political conspiracies unusual, not only in coups d'état or political assassinations, but also in more harmless situations, such as the struggle for political positions.[30] Time and again, people conspire in secret to achieve things that cannot be achieved in open, transparent and democratic ways. Conspiracies are no different.

Conspiracies are a common issue for the law. A conspiracy theory, in the literal sense of the word, is nothing more than a criminal investigative hypothesis. In the case of police and public prosecutors, such hypotheses are a part of professional working life and are an "indispensable basis ... for clarification and evidence," according to a standard forensic textbook.[31] There is no other way to combat the corresponding criminality since crimes, especially those involving several perpetrators, rarely happen by chance. Conspiracies are supposed to work and therefore they are planned. Investigators must draw up theories about the nature of these plans, which could then prove to be either false or verifiable in the course of investigation. So simple, so banal.

It is no coincidence that the word conspiracy refers to the plan to commit a crime. A conspiracy is a prosecutable criminal offence in both the UK and the US.[32] Thus, a conspiracy theory in these countries always implies that the perpetrators are criminals who should be brought to justice. The word does not have these criminal dimensions in Germany, although the situation is similarly punishable. Paragraph 129 of the German Criminal Code (Formation of Criminal Associations) states that "those who participate as members in an association whose purpose or activity is directed towards the commission of criminal offences" will be punished. According to Paragraph 30 (relating to the attempt to participate), "anyone who conspires with another to commit a crime" will also be punished. However, this standard is seldom applied in the German courts and charges are rarely pressed.[33]

But the exact meaning of a conspiracy theory as "a presumption of conspiracy to commit a criminal offence" has little to do with how the term is actually used today. It is usually not a question of true or false, or even an open-ended search for evidence. Rather, conspiracy theories are generally interpreted as delusional from the outset, and thus as a special category of stupid and unenlightened, if not pathological, thinking. This shift in meaning is remarkable and rarely discussed. In today's common use of the word, conspiracy theories cannot be proven to be true or false: They are false by definition, even before they are verified.[34] American media scientist Jack Bratich writes:

"Conspiracy theories do not reach the threshold of acceptability to even be tested, to be falsifiable. If the mind is that sphere that can distinguish between truth and falsity, then conspiracy theories are beyond that sphere. They are para (beyond or beside) the nous (mind). They are paranoid."[35]

Those who accuse others, such as the "coronavirus demonstrators," of spreading such views, consider themselves to be mentally healthier, wiser, and more enlightened. Since conspiracy theories are considered to be "paranoid nonsense," it is assumed that there is no need to go into their details. This is also unadvisable because conspiracy theorists are considered to be unteachable, meaning a discussion with them is a waste of time.

However, these critics say that such theories cannot merely be dismissed as absurd quirks. Especially in times of crisis, they would be extremely dangerous. They would lead to general distrust and doubts about the good intentions of the government and the elite in general. If this distrust of those at the top continues to be fueled and eventually boils over, the country would become unbalanced and be in danger of sinking into chaos.

For this reason, those who are still open to rational arguments would have to be enlightened about these dangers. And the rest, those who have already drifted too far, would have to be vigorously contested and banished from the public debate arena so that their "poison" does not continue to have a destructive effect on society.

The attitude outlined here is widespread, especially among intellectuals and opinion leaders. It is based on a number of basic assumptions that are rarely openly mentioned. These include:

→ The established system is basically a good system.
→ People who think differently are often less intelligent.
→ People need guidance, especially when forming opinions.

Among these assumptions, which are deeply woven into the conspiracy theory debate (so deeply that many people seem not to even be aware of them), one thing above all stands out: their authoritarian character. Liberalism, pluralism and democracy would, in fact, take the exact opposite position:

→ The established order should be called into question.
→ People who think differently could be smarter.
→ People should use their intelligence without being instructed by others.

Therefore, the debate on conspiracy theories will also always be a debate about one's own particular political understanding and view of the human condition. The great counterhypothesis of the conspiracy theory alarmists is that political conspiracies are fundamentally implausible, that no one conspires, and that almost everything is either a coincidence or the result of chaotic, uncontrollable developments. The adherents of this view could thus be described as "chance theorists" insofar as they explain the course of the world without hidden, behind-the-scenes planning.

It is striking that these chance theorists are much closer to the conspiracy theorists in thought than they would believe. For the blanket rejection of conspiracy theories is, as already mentioned in the previous chapter, *structurally similar* to the fundamental belief in conspiracy theories. Both thought processes are two sides of the same coin: an expression of the same desire for unambiguousness.

There is a great misunderstanding in this desire for clarity. The world is neither clearly planned nor clearly chaotic, but rather it is a dazzling, immeasurably multi-layered, never completely comprehensible web of constantly emerging and dissolving alliances, of conflicting interests, of strategic plans and of unfortunate (or fortunate) coincidences. This meshwork includes coincidences *and* conspiracies.

Secret intrigues are also not always vast "global conspiracies." Sometimes they last only a few days and have a specific, easily achievable goal. Sometimes, however, they persist for decades without being uncovered.[36] Conspiracies are not always successful: many fail. But if they don't fail, and this is precisely the point, then they remain inherently secret and thus invisible. Thus, at the risk of sounding trivial, whoever is honestly interested in knowledge should always look closely at the facts behind every conspiracy theory. It is not only unwise but downright foolish to exclude something from the outset because it doesn't fit with one's own world view and calls into question convictions to which one feels connected.

A complex event like the coronavirus crisis cannot be understood, or perhaps can only be superficially grasped, as long as one prohibits oneself, or others, from having conspiratorial thoughts from the outset. Chance theorists often display a particular weakness of thought. They tend to accept the given as proven and to accept the superficial as the truth: "Everything is as it appears to be." They accept whatever the recognized authorities, including government ministers, mainstream media, or appointed professors, state as the truth, without expressing any doubt. Therefore, they are in a position to be more easily deceived by these authorities—more easily than they themselves, in particular, believe.

A well-known example of this is the *New York Times* journalist Judith Miller (who reappears in Chapter 3), who, in her articles, repeatedly disseminated unverified information that had been leaked to her by intelligence services and that played an important role in the run-up to the 2003 Iraq War. She openly confessed her conviction that it was not her job to question internal information from government circles. After all, she herself could not be an independent intelligence agency. This left her dependent on the authorities for information. Her role was to simply tell readers about those ideas that were circulating within the government.[37]

This kind of trust, which could also be described as a mixture of convenience and opportunism, is widespread in the mainstream media, even if few admit it as openly as Judith Miller.

Conspiracy theoretical thinking is more curious, more suspicious; it scratches beneath the surface, wants to find out more, and suspects deception, particularly on the part of the authorities. One weakness of this thinking lies in its exaggeration of causality. It tends to causally link together ideas that might only be loosely connected. Another weakness of conspiracy theoretical thinking lies in its negativity. Whereas chance theorists live in a relatively intact world (which they do not want to have destroyed), conspiracy theorists are often just one step ahead of the apocalypse, and are therefore chronically depressed, discontent, and alarmist.

Perhaps the alternative is a synthesis, a combination of both ways of thinking, in which the stubborn, critical curiosity of the conspiracy theorists fuses with the trusting optimism of the chance theorists. In this way, the deep divide created with great effort in recent years could finally be bridged, with emphasis on a fundamental commonality—the mutual interest in insight and knowledge.

It must be possible to agree on this, because without a joint striving for knowledge and truth, not only science (and medicine in particular) will sacrifice its effectiveness and degenerate into a commercial tool for those with influence, but the justice system will also lose its meaning and mutate into a haggling among the powerful (with the keyword being international arbitration).[38] Power, money, and corruption have always been great adversaries of the quest for knowledge, not just in science and justice, but also in culture, politics, and the media. Wherever newspapers and television stations are the property of billionaires or are involved in undemocratic power structures, the search for truth will always be disadvantaged.

Only an awareness of shared insights, the common interest of all human beings, will keep society united and drive its progress. When, however, individual areas of knowledge, whether in medicine or in politics, are undermined as absurd, this acts as a brake on social development. Prohibiting questionable knowledge and excluding it from discussion does not serve the purpose of enlightenment, but rather paralyzes everyone, undermining their intelligence.

In its extreme, such a mental stalemate creates the assumption that the rich and influential, in conjunction with politics, only want the best for society. This rhetoric, which has been in vogue for some time, if it is successful and believed by the majority, can be compared to a blinding of the intellect. It threatens the critical mind itself. In other words, whoever believes this becomes incapable of questioning information and is, from a democratic perspective, neutralized as a political citizen.

Conspiracy theories that question the harmonious narrative of coherence from top to bottom develop, in such situations, into a means of mental self-defense. They should be thoroughly scrutinized and verified without prejudice—with a curious interest in knowledge, but without fearing the apocalypse.

2

Biosecurity and the Politics of Fear

Before beginning with the chronicle of events that the title of this book refers to, we need to take a look behind the scenes of the actual setting. Viruses and epidemics are a scientific and politically specialized area with their own experts and institutions, and a history of their own.

Almost everyone is now familiar with the Johns Hopkins University, which daily provides the entire world with the latest numbers of those who have tested positive for the virus. Many also know that in October 2019, just a few weeks before the outbreak of the crisis, the Johns Hopkins Center for Health Security had organized an exercise entitled Event 201 in which an astonishingly similar scenario was played out (see Chapter 6).

Less well-known is the fact that the Center for Health Security, although it has been operating for more than twenty years, has only been operating under this name since 2013. The institution was established in 1998 as the Center for Civilian Biodefense Strategies. In 2003 the name was changed to the Center for Biosecurity, before eventually being changed again to the Center for Health Security. In their external representation, therefore, a rather military sounding name was modified to the more innocuous sounding "Health Security." Irrespective of the name changes, the Center has been one the most important international organizations when it comes to public debate on the dangers of bioweapons and epidemics.

In order to understand what has been happening in the world since the beginning of 2020, and how and why such a crisis was actually foretold—especially by this Center—it is helpful to first understand both the terminology used and its context.

The term "biosecurity" has become increasingly popular in politics and science in recent years. It refers to a diffuse and ambiguous field of research in which military policies and science merge. To give a little-known example: German Federal Health Minister Jens Spahn created a new Department for Health Security at the beginning of 2020, the establishment of which had already been planned for at the end of 2019.[39] This department is headed by Hans-Ulrich Holtherm, a general in the Bundeswehr (the German armed forces) who had previously led a newly-established NATO agency that dealt with the "early detection of infectious disease outbreaks in near real time," as well as with the "centralized surveillance of the deployed forces."[40] Holtherm continues to wear a uniform in his current position at the Ministry of Health, where he heads the coronavirus crisis team and advises Jens Spahn on crisis management.[41] With this fusion of medicine and military, the Minister of Health is on-trend.

Biosecurity means protection against pandemics and attacks with bioweapons, i.e., against viruses, bacteria and poisons. Numerous simulation exercises have been carried out in recent years, pandemic plans have been developed, and structures for crisis management have been created. All this is now becoming partially visible in the coronavirus crisis and points to a history that is as long as it is disturbing. The planning for protection from danger has often gone hand in hand with the creation of precisely that threat—in other words, the development of weapons of mass destruction.

The word biosecurity is, itself, a propaganda term, an expression that conveys a concealed message. It assumes that all social groups have a common interest in a crisis situation, namely security. But it is not that simple.[42] A bioweapon attack or an outbreak of the disease means different things to different groups:

→ For the public, it is a frightening, deadly threat.
→ For the government, it is a crisis in which it is under pressure or in which it can distinguish itself as the protector.
→ For the pharmaceutical industry, it is a profitable new field of business.
→ For the military, it is an opportunity to investigate a potentially useful weapon.

Exactly where the science stands on this list depends on to whom the researchers are committed—or financially obliged: the public, the government, the pharmaceutical industry, or the military. Such obligations can, of course, overlap. But it would be reckless and naive to presume that all participants view the subject with the same interest and therefore also strive for a common goal without contradiction—specifically the often invoked "biosecurity."

The military aspect in particular has been of great importance for a long time, but this is not something that is often talked about readily and openly:

"We have here weapons that could be very cheap, that could be particularly suitable for attacking large populations, and which place a premium on the sudden, surprise attack. ... You could almost not ask for a better description of what the United States should not want to see happen to the art of war. And yet of all the countries in the world it is the United States which conspicuously pioneers in this area."[43]

This assessment of biological weapons is more than fifty years old and is attributed to Matthew Meselson, one of the world's most renowned microbiologists. Meselson, a professor at Harvard since 1960, who is still there to this day, advised the US government on disarmament issues in the 1960s and contributed significantly to getting the Biological Weapons Convention adopted by the UN in 1972 and signed by the US. In this resolution, the signatory countries undertook "never in any circumstances to develop, produce, stockpile or otherwise acquire or retain" biological weapons.[44]

In the late 1960s, when Meselson issued his warning, it gradually came to light how deeply the US government was involved in research programs to develop biological and chemical weapons.[45] Since the 1940s, much of the research has been carried out at the Fort Detrick military base about an hour's drive north of Washington DC, which is still today the headquarters of military research into dangerous pathogens.

It only became known many years later that immediately after the Second World War the US government had recruited many high-ranking German scientists, including Walter Schreiber, Kurt Blome and Erich Traub, who had previously researched bioweapons for the Nazis and, in some cases, were also responsible for human experiments in the concentration camps. They shared their knowledge of bacteria and viruses and their ability to use them in the fight against humans.[46] The US also resorted to using Japanese experts after the war. Officer Ishii Shiro, the head of the notorious Unit 731 of the Imperial Japanese Army, and his collaborators, who performed human experiments on thousands of prisoners in occupied China, gained immunity from prosecution helped by the celebrated US general and war hero Douglas McArthur in return for the Japanese officer's knowledge of information on the viability of biological weapons.[47]

Money was available in plentiful amounts: In the 1960s, the US government spent hundreds of millions of dollars on research into biological and chemical weapons and also the defense against them.[48] Several of the programs (for example, Project 112) were so secret that their existence was denied for several decades and not officially acknowledged until 2000.[49] Much is still under lock and key.

More than 500 scientists researched deadly germs at Fort Detrick in 1968 and more than 700,000 animals, including pigs and monkeys, were killed in experiments each year (!).[50] More than 5,000 US soldiers were exposed to pathogens in experiments, not all knowingly.[51]

Serious accidents also occurred. In the spring of 1968, the military used an aircraft over the state of Utah to spray the nerve agent VX for testing purposes, and, due to a technical failure in closing the poison tanks, accidentally killed more than 6,000 grazing sheep.[52] It was pure coincidence that the wind changed direction an hour later and no people were killed.[53]

Two years earlier, in June 1966, military scientists distributed disease-causing bacteria in the New York subway system to measure their spread. The New York authorities were not informed and the experiment only became public many years later.[54]

In the 1950s and 1960s, bacteria were sprayed from military aircraft above populated areas in the US and Canada (Operation LAC) to measure their dispersion. The aim was to find out how biological weapons could be used against an enemy, such as the Soviet Union, in the event of war.[55]

Within the framework of the research for a new weapon that combined biological pathogens with nuclear radiation during the Cold War, residents in poor neighborhoods in US cities like

St. Louis were deliberately exposed to disease by pathogens that were sprayed from the rooftops. Those affected have reported the subsequent development of cancers.[56]

In Nashville in the late 1940s, 800 pregnant women from poor backgrounds were, without their knowledge, given a mixture containing radioactive iron during a medical examination. The researchers then took blood tests to determine how much of the radioactive substance was absorbed by the mothers and babies. Similar tests were also conducted in San Francisco and Chicago.[57]

The author Lisa Martino-Taylor, who discovered these facts over many years of researching documents, subsequently publishing them in a book[58] on the same subject in 2017 to correlate with her doctoral thesis,[59] and which led to questions from several congressional representatives, commented on these attempts by the government:

"They targeted the most vulnerable in society in most cases. They targeted children. They targeted pregnant women in Nashville. People who were ill in hospitals. And they targeted minority populations."[60]

Large areas of the country, and especially those with the most vulnerable of its citizens, involuntarily and secretly became part of a research trial. How many people became ill or died as a result of this experiment has never been investigated.

This type of research on biological weapons became officially taboo in the US after 1969. From then on, only "defensive" research was supposed to be carried out, i.e., for antidotes in defense against an attack. However, after the adoption of the Biological Weapons Convention, there was never an agreement on an additional binding protocol that would have established a mechanism for international control. After lengthy negotiations, the US government rejected such a protocol in July 2001.[61] Thus, there is still no formal procedure for verifying compliance with the Convention in the individual states. The German Federal Agency for Civic Education writes:

"One problem with the Bioweapons Convention is that it explicitly allows work with biological microorganisms and toxic agents that could be used as weapons as long as they are 'justified by preventive, protective, or other peaceful purposes' (Article I). This will enable work to be done on bioweapon defenses, which means research into both existing and possible future bioweapons. In this way, defense research could also be misused for the development of new bioweapons."[62]

In this opaque grey area of danger prevention and danger production, a biological arms race began with Moscow during the Cold War where the Soviet military was conducting very similar research. The political situation changed fundamentally in the 1990s. After the disintegration of the Soviet Union and the Eastern Bloc, the Western military apparatus lost its enemy, which meant existential danger for the entire sector. Even more dangerous than the Russian military was the sector's own uselessness.

How could the multibillion-dollar spending for the army, navy, air force, CIA, NSA, and the rest of the dozen US intelligence agencies be justified in the future? Who still needed fighter jets, aircraft carriers, nuclear missiles, and the additional arsenal that had been acquired to keep communism at bay now that East and West were at peace and could disarm safely? This question has been raised with great urgency since 1990 by many politicians, the military, intelligence agencies, and arms and defense contractors, who, in previous decades had, in the words of US President Eisenhower, merged into a "military-industrial complex,"[63] a powerful force that largely guided not only the US but also international politics.[64]

The answer was obvious and has always been the same: Armament requires fear. A population that fears no enemies will not accept the expenditure of billions on the military. When communism disappeared, a new enemy was needed to take its place. Colin Powell, the then Chairman of the Joint Chiefs of Staff, and thus the most senior military officer in the United States, put it quite frankly, and with some sarcasm, in an interview in the spring of 1991:

> "I'm running out of demons. I'm running out of villains. I'm down to Castro and Kim Il Sung."[65]

In this context, the threat of terrorism came increasingly into focus in the 1990s. And together with this, came warnings of the threat of attacks using biological weapons. The 1994 National Security Strategy adopted by President Bill Clinton was intended to prevent more countries from obtaining chemical, biological, and nuclear weapons. If this failed, however, the US should be in a position to "be able to deter, prevent and defend itself against the use of such weapons."[66] It was primarily aimed at the concern that weapons of mass destruction from the stocks of the crumbling Soviet Union and its successor states could fall into the "wrong hands." But the focus of the effort expanded rapidly.

In February 1995, Joe Biden, then chairman of the US Senate Committee on the Judiciary, introduced a major bill in the US Senate to "enable a better response to an international terrorist threat."[67] The plan met with fierce opposition, including from civil rights groups, who viewed it as restricting constitutional rights.[68] The bill remained controversial and its passage seemed uncertain.

This changed abruptly a few weeks later after an event that would characterize politics for years to come: the bombing of a government building in Oklahoma City on April 19, 1995. With 168 dead and 700 injured, this was considered the most serious terrorist attack in the history of the country at the time. Not only was the new anti-terrorism act passed quickly and without further discussion, the president also assured the public that intelligence agencies and investigative authorities would receive increased access to information and funding. From this point on, public debate focused on the threat of terrorism. In the face of the devastating bombing, it was clear to everyone why protection from radical extremists was so important. After all, it could affect anyone anywhere, not only in foreign crisis areas, but also in a very normal city in the Midwest.

The attack changed public perception on the subject in a lasting way. Its background, however, remained opaque. Many questions about the alleged assassin, Timothy McVeigh, a highly decorated Gulf War veteran who, according to his own statement, had become an informer in a secret special forces unit in the army to infiltrate the neo-Nazi scene after his return from the war, remain unanswered.[69] The original trail to other perpetrators was never pursued.

In June 1995, shortly after the attack, Clinton issued a special anti-terrorism directive that redirected the attention of all government agencies to the danger of the newly determined terrorist threat.[70] The US was to have "no higher priority" in the future than the prevention of terrorists from accessing biological and other weapons of mass destruction. Appropriate emergency plans would be reviewed and tested. The main governmental departments, together with the CIA and the FBI, would have to submit a joint "Counterterrorism Readiness Report" to the president. Terrorism became the government's key issue.

In the months and years that followed, additional measures were implemented to further consolidate this policy. Studies were commissioned, conferences were organized, and hearings were held by Congress. In a long article in a major newspaper in 1997, two political strategists, James Woolsey (former head of the CIA) and Joseph Nye (former Assistant Secretary of Defense who coined the term "soft power") warned under the headline "Defend Against the Shadow Enemy":

> "The destruction of the Federal Building in Oklahoma City and the bombing of the World Trade Center in New York shocked Americans. But those tragedies would have been far worse if nuclear, biological or chemical materials had been involved. After co-chairing a year-long study for the government, we believe it is increasingly likely they will be. ...
>
> "Terrorists worldwide have better access to anthrax or sarin than to nuclear materials. So far we have been lucky. But we should not wait for another Pearl Harbor to awaken us to the fact that there is no greater threat to our security than terrorism involving weapons of mass destruction. ...
>
> "But recent years have seen the rise of a new type of terrorists [sic] less interested in promoting a political cause and more focused on retribution or eradication of what they define as evil. Their motives are often a distorted form of religion and their imagined rewards are in the next world."[71]

This text, which is representative of the then established anti-terrorist campaign of a military and political elite, contained a number of subtext messages. On the one hand, the keyword "Pearl Harbor" was used to touch on a national trauma of vulnerability and defenselessness that aroused deep emotions in many Americans. On the other hand, the authors characterized the new enemy as faceless (a "shadow" enemy), irrational, blinded and full of longing for death. It logically followed that negotiating with this enemy would be impossible, thus increasing the threat. This nameless, bioterrorist enemy embodied evil itself.

In the same year, US Secretary of Defense William Cohen held an ordinary packet of sugar in front of the camera on a national television morning show, silencing the thus far cheerful hosts with the single word "anthrax":

> "If Saddam Hussein spread this amount of anthrax over a city the size of, say, Washington, D.C., it would destroy at least half the population of that city. One breath, and you are likely to face death within five days."[72]

This fearmongering also promoted a planned government program to vaccinate the more than two million US soldiers against anthrax, which, however, was later only partially implemented.[73] Many soldiers reported severe side effects.[74] The journalist Maureen Dowd commented sarcastically on Cohen's television performance with the sugar packet at the time:

> "In an era when people care more about stocks than politics, the notion that Washington might disappear has made it relevant again. Suddenly there are fears about Iraqi crop dusters spraying death on the Mall, about the nation's

capital being another Nagasaki. It was a flashback to the days of bomb shelters and learning to crawl under your desk if the big one hit."[75]

At the same time, government researchers were working in secret on powerful bioweapons. The CIA developed a biological bomb as part of Project Clear Vision in 1997 and investigated how exactly the pathogens would spread when they were used.[76] The Defense Intelligence Agency (DIA) began manufacturing a genetically engineered version of the deadly anthrax bacteria in the same year (Project Jefferson) that was so secret that those involved said the White House was "probably" in the dark about it.[77] When this bioweapons development was later reported in the press, a Pentagon spokeswoman said that the project was fully in accord with the UN Biological Weapons Convention because the research was of a purely defensive nature.[78]

Parallel to this, the first behind-the-scenes training was launched to test how the government would react to a bioterrorist attack. In the spring of 1998, forty representatives of various agencies met in Washington.[79] Things had become specific. According to the run-through scenario, terrorists had spread a modified smallpox virus in California for which there were no treatment possibilities. Panic quickly erupted in the wake of the rapid spreading of the fictitious smallpox virus and there was disagreement over the responsibilities of those involved. The conclusion of this test: The government was unprepared and therefore gravely endangered. The *New York Times* reported on its front page in alarm: "Exercise Finds U.S. Unable to Handle Germ War Threat."[80] This was the message that was subsequently widely spread. Even the president himself must have felt that he was in danger; in the summer of 1998, the FBI revealed that terrorists from Texas had announced that they were planning to kill Clinton using a bioweapon.[81]

In the same year, Clinton signed sweeping orders in which the position of National Coordinator for Security, Infrastructure Protection and Counter-Terrorism was created and where, simultaneously, all public agencies were to develop plans to protect critical infrastructure, specifically in the form of public-private partnerships with the participation of private companies.[82] This energized counterterrorism campaign opened up numerous new and profitable fields of business.

Foreign policy also became increasingly important. In 1997, the Project for the New American Century was founded: a lobbying group that developed considerable influence in promoting a more aggressive foreign policy and increased military-spending. The group, including many ex-members of the Reagan administration who were waiting out the Clinton period but would soon resume leadership positions under George W. Bush, declared that its main objective was to "increase defense spending significantly" to "carry out our global responsibilities."[83]

In 1998, the initiators wrote a letter to President Clinton in which he was pressed to "remove" the Iraqi government under Saddam Hussein from power—a "difficult, but necessary project" in which Clinton was assured "full support." This call for a coup or war was justified by Saddam's possession of weapons of mass destruction, in particular chemical and biological weapons whose existence could not actually be proven but could also not be ruled out.[84] The letter, signed by nearly twenty political heavyweights, including the abovementioned ex-CIA chief James Woolsey and future Vice President Dick Cheney, could be viewed as a barely-veiled threat to Clinton; if he did not switch to the desired course of war, he would have a powerful alliance working against him.

This challenge reached Clinton at a particularly delicate, personal time: in January 1998, just days after the Lewinsky scandal (Clinton's sexual affair with his intern Monica Lewinsky) had broken in the media. The president was quick to accommodate the lobby group. The successful negotiations of the UN weapons inspectors with Iraq were sabotaged by the US and Clinton ordered a multi-faceted bombing attack of the country that was already suffering badly under economic sanctions,[85] all in the same year. This episode was a precursor to the 2003 Iraq War.

Soon after this, the Project for the New American Century launched the publication *Rebuilding America's Defenses: Strategies, Forces and Resources for a New Century*. The ninety-page document was published in September 2000 in the midst of the presidential campaign that was then being fought between Clinton's vice president Al Gore and George W. Bush. The aim of the study was to explain to the next government, whether under Gore or Bush, that the military would have to be radically redesigned and that military-spending, in particular on new weapons' research, should be increased urgently in order for the US to remain number one in the world in the coming decades.

The document was full of military fantasies of domination. Its primary author was Thomas Donnelly, a former senior official on the US House of Representatives' Committee on National Security and later the director of strategic communications and initiatives at Lockheed Martin. (An aside: Donnelly openly confessed to secretly living a double life as a woman. In 2018 he transitioned, taking the name Giselle Donnelly, and has since openly confessed to having a sadomasochistic relationship with an ex-officer of the US Navy.[86]) Donnelly's study has often been cited. Published a year before 9/11, it stated that a "catastrophic and catalyzing event—like a new Pearl Harbor," would significantly facilitate the recommended radical reform of the military.[87] It also stated, with a view to the future:

"The art of warfare on air, land, and sea will be vastly different than it is today, and 'combat' likely will take place in new dimensions: in space, 'cyber-space,' and perhaps the world of microbes. ... And advanced forms of biological warfare that can 'target' specific genotypes may transform biological warfare from the realm of terror to a politically useful tool."[88]

Since a half dozen high-ranking US military officers also participated in the preparation of the publication and discussion, it can be assumed that such thoughts were being considered in these circles. In fact, one of the senior bioweapons experts in the US military had drafted a strategy paper in 1995 that stated:

"Biological warfare offers ... the only weapon of mass destruction which has utility across the spectrum of conflict. Using biological weapons under the cover of an endemic or natural disease occurrence provides an attacker the potential for plausible denial. In this context, biological weapons offer greater possibilities for use than do nuclear weapons. ... Biological weapons can be employed in non-combat settings under the guise of natural events, during operations other than war, or can be used in open combat scenarios against all biological systems—man, animal or plant. ... In addition, the problem of biological warfare cannot be narrowly focused on its ability to kill or render people ill. Biological warfare's potential to create significant economic loss and subsequent political instability with plausible denial exceeds any other known weapon."[89]

The author, Robert Kadlec, a former officer in the Special Forces and a bioweapons inspector for the US military in Iraq, wanted this description to be understood as a warning of possible plans by enemies of the US. The fact that he repeatedly emphasized the possibility of a plausible denial of such a covert use of weapons in his paper, however, at least made readers pay attention. Kadlec later had a stellar career. In 2007, under President George W. Bush, he became the government's chief adviser on biodefense, and in 2017 he became Assistant Secretary for Preparedness and Response at the US Department of Health and Human Services. In this capacity, he signed a two billion-dollar contract for the delivery of a smallpox vaccine to a pharmaceutical company that he had previously served as a consultant.[90] In the coronavirus crisis, he became one of the US government's senior crisis managers.[91]

What remains to be noted: In the 1990s, the issues of terrorism and of bioweapons were developed, with considerable effort and great consistency, into a politically usable tool to fill the space created by the disappearance of communism. The great enemy in Moscow was replaced by many small "rogues" and faceless "bioterrorists" who had to be kept at bay in the interests of national security. What remained was the basic principle: Instill fear in the population in order to gain political maneuverability.

3

Dark Winter:
A State of Emergency is Tested
(1998–2001)

1998 saw the creation of another institution that has since played a key role in keeping and continuously developing the topic of biosecurity on the political agenda. This is the abovementioned Johns Hopkins Center for Civilian Biodefense Strategies, now called the Center for Health Security, which has taken a leading role in the coronavirus crisis. Over the past twenty years, the Center has become a hub of scientific conferences, emergency exercises, and, most importantly, the continued dissemination of scaremongering issues to the public. It was here that researchers, military leaders and politicians would meet, and it was here that plans and guidelines were developed that soon became influential worldwide.

If one looks at how the Center is financed and who its sponsoring organizations are, it becomes clear how much American research depends on private donors. The Center received its initial funding from the Johns Hopkins School of Public Health, which itself was established in 1916 by the billionaire John D. Rockefeller's foundation as part of Johns Hopkins University, which, in turn, had been established in 1876 by a large donation from the billionaire Johns Hopkins. These influences and circumstances are not merely issues that belong in the past. In 2001, the School of Public Health extended its name to the Bloomberg School of Public Health, after Michael Bloomberg, one of the wealthiest people in the world—and a candidate for the US presidency in 2020—donated a total of more than three billion (!) dollars to the Johns Hopkins University.

Bloomberg, Rockefeller, Hopkins—whatever these extremely wealthy persons and those they choose as employees deem important, is what receives research funding. Their influence on the organizations and institutions they support is commensurate with the size of their donations. The problem is not only that, thanks to their immense wealth, these people are able to make their privately acquired views the standard version of social wisdom, it is also problematic that such wealthy philanthropists like to support those things that, in the long run, are both advantageous and profitable to their own companies or the companies of their friends.

Those who donate billions to research have a decisive influence on the advancement of certain branches of science and create impulses and trends that politicians then take up and further reinforce with their own funding. There is a qualitative difference between donating a hundred thousand dollars for a specific purpose or a hundred million dollars. While a hundred thousand dollars may be added as support for a specific budget, a hundred million dollars can determine a whole new direction in which other donors then orient themselves.

In its early years, the Center for Civilian Biodefense Strategies received money from various superrich benefactors, including the foundation of billionaire Alfred Sloan. In praise of the benefactor, the Center says:

> "When Sloan got involved in 2000, the professional field of biosecurity did not exist. There was little science or scholarship no guidelines or planning tools, and few policies or officials to direct civilian preparedness, planning, and

response. Over ten years, the Sloan Foundation awarded more than $44 million in biosecurity grants and was instrumental in establishing the field and many of its most prominent leaders. That was money well-invested. The nation is now vastly better prepared for bioterrorism and other catastrophic threats to the public's health and national security."[92]

The cash flow at the time was arranged by Ralph Gomory, chairman of the Sloan Foundation. Gomory, the son of a politically influential banker, was a mathematician, longtime vice president of the computer company IBM, member of the Council on Foreign Relations, and board member of the Washington Post Company, the Bank of New York, and a pharmaceutical company.

This list is intended to show that such foundation investments are decided by people who come from a cross-section of industry elite whose internal discussions do not always enter public consciousness. Unlike in democratic decision-making processes of publicly funded institutions, money managers in private foundations are solely accountable to their financiers. Foundations are thus naturally shaped by the spirit and private goals of their founders. Alfred Sloan (1875–1966) was one of the most influential industrialists of his time, best known for his anti-unionism and his focus on entrepreneurial efficiency, in which humanity was overlooked. From the 1930s to the 1950s, he was the head of General Motors, a company that, under his leadership before and during World War II, was one of the world's largest suppliers of armaments, ironically to both the US and Nazi Germany. Sloan made money on both sides of the war.[93]

However, it would be too easy to generally conclude that private foundations pursue "evil goals," deliberately cause harm, or are part of a conspiracy. As part of a structure based on competition and enrichment, and in which power is increasingly concentrated, they tend to reproduce their own structures and values, their own flawed "operating system," again and again. What is missing is a corrective mechanism via a democratic public. Foundations can do whatever their owners like and ignore the rest, but they have a profound impact on politics and society.[94]

The foundations, their managers, and their financiers tend to overestimate their own wisdom and equate their own interests with those of the country by mere virtue of their size and power. There is a famous quote from Charles Wilson, the successor to Alfred Sloan at the helm of General Motors, who was appointed US Secretary of Defense in 1953 and who responded to a senator's question about whether his large holding of shares in the company might lead to a conflict of interest in political decisions:

> "I cannot conceive of one [situation like that] because for years I thought what was good for our country was good for General Motors, and vice versa. The difference did not exist. Our company is too big. It goes with the welfare of the country. Our contribution to the Nation is quite considerable. ... I cannot conceive of it. I do not think we are going to get into any foolishness like seizing the properties or anything like that, you know, like the Iranians are in over there ... I would like to tell you men there is a change in the country. The people are not afraid of businessmen like me right now."[95]

Today, these could be the words of Bill Gates or the Amazon CEO, Jeff Bezos. They reflect an institutionalized corruption that becomes unassailable when the public allows themselves to be governed by corporate executives.

Whether it is the tech savvy, efficiency-obsessed billionaire Sloan, the mathematician and industry manager Gomory, who subsequently managed the billions that Sloan's foundation left behind, or, more recently, Bill Gates, all are convinced that what they are doing is good. However, they are viewing the world with their specifically-oriented tunnel vision and, because of their social separation from the "normal" population, they only focus on those problems relevant to their own sphere. Child poverty, educational injustice or the state of crisis in the care of the elderly are hardly ever mentioned, because these people and their families and friends are not affected by such existential concerns and because they presumably do not affect the operational security of the entire system, but "only" the quality of life of the people "below" them.

The situation is different, however, when it comes to bioterrorism and epidemics; these perils potentially also threaten elites and their corporations. At the turn of the millennium, when Gomory decided to help the biosecurity field achieve a breakthrough, he seemed genuinely concerned about a possible future terrorist attack using biological weapons.

The first conference organized by the Center for Civilian Biodefense Strategies took place in February 1999, half a year after its founding, and its size was impressive—more than 900 participants from ten countries had traveled to Washington to the Crystal Gateway Marriott, not far from the Pentagon, in order to participate in two days of discussions on bioterrorism.[96] The gathering included members of the military, bureaucrats, and aspiring researchers, who, in addition to worrying about an attack, also shared something else: Biosecurity was an issue that could secure their livelihoods. If they were able to make the importance of this danger clear to both the politicians and the public, research and project funds would be secured for years to come together with the creation of completely new institutions and departments in which it would be possible to find permanent work. It was clear to all involved that there was potential.

This was also true for the pharmaceutical industry. Richard Clarke, National Coordinator for Security, Infrastructure Protection and Counter-terrorism, whose office had been created only a few months earlier in response to the new fixation on terror, told the conference:

> "For the first time the Department of Health and Human Services is part of the national security apparatus of the United States. The current bioterrorism initiative includes a new concept: the first-ever procurement of specialized medicines for a national civilian protection stockpile. As new vaccines and medicines are developed, that program can be expanded. The initiative includes invigoration of research and development in the science of biodefense; it invests in pathogen genome sequencing, new vaccine research, new therapeutics research, and development of improved detection and diagnostic systems."[97]

In other words, a huge market for new products and treatments was opening up, all coupled with national security, and thus given the highest priority by the government.

At the conference, presentations were made on why the newly-recognized danger was genuine and not exaggerated, where the threat would arise (Iraq, US citizen militia groups), and which pathogens would most likely be used (smallpox, anthrax). Colonel Gerald Parker, head of military bioweapons (defense) research at Fort Detrick, explained that it was easy to determine which bacteria and viruses terrorists could use to build the most effective bioweapons—one need only look at which bioweapons the US itself had been researching until the official ban in 1969.[98]

What remains doubtful is how much actual compliance, if any, the ban had. In 1999, the same year that the conference took place, the Pentagon had secretly built a production plant for the manufacture of anthrax in the Nevada desert, specifying that all components should be standard issue and generally accessible (Project Bacchus).[99] After many months of intensive work, the researchers were successful. Apparently, they had wanted to determine whether terrorists without access to advanced technology would be able to achieve the same thing. Admittedly, the project also made it theoretically possible to carry out an anthrax attack as a false-flag operation, where it would appear as if the weapons had been made and used by amateur nonprofessionals. The alleged dividing line between offensive and defensive bioweapon research, between defense and deception, had been lost in an opaque gray zone.

On the second day of the conference, the participants acted out a prepared, elaborately complex scenario, where undefined terrorists attacked a fictional northeastern US town with smallpox. The seven-page plan described a detailed progression of the crisis as it developed over a period of two months.[100] The catastrophe was described vividly and graphically; the text read like a film script. The exercise became particularly realistic due to the fact that the roles of medical and political protagonists were performed at the conference by participants who also had real-life responsibilities in their respective institutions. Some passages of the 1999 evaluation report sound similar to the current coronavirus crisis:

"How to control the message going to the public weighs heavily upon the minds of all panelists. ... Official channels will not be the only source of information during the epidemic, argues the public affairs specialist. ... Controlling the message that goes out over the airwaves could be extremely difficult, especially since there may not even be any consensus on what the message should be in the first place. Several panelists point out the need to ensure that information presented to the media is consistent and credible. ...

"The distribution of antibiotics and vaccines represents a logistical problem that must be overcome. ... Tens of thousands of people are vaccinated, but many more still need vaccine. ... A consensus must be reached as to how to proceed with the vaccinations. ... According to a 1905 Massachusetts case, cites a state's assistant attorney general, compulsory vaccinations are not a violation of due process and are therefore legal. So the local, state, and federal levels of government have no obstacle to vaccinating those designated at risk. ...

"How far can police go to detain quarantined patients? The limits of emergency powers should be clearly delineated in any predisaster planning. ... Should the city have been placed under immediate quarantine? Should martial law have been implemented?"[101]

The practice simulation, in which unrest finally breaks out, the National Guard is called for help, and the mayor suffers a heart attack, concludes with the words:

"Without vaccine, the only control method is isolation, which hinders, but cannot halt, the spread of the disease. By year's end, endemic smallpox is reestablished in 14 countries."[102]

In November 2000, the same group of officials from the various agencies met again for a second major conference on the same subject.[103] Financial problems had been resolved with receipt of the first payment of millions from the Sloan Foundation.[104] This time, the fictional city was called Goodtown, and rather than smallpox, it was affected by the plague. Again, unspecified terrorists were responsible. This time, however, the terrorist aspect was clearly a background issue. The simulation exercise was headlined "Epidemic Response Scenario: Decision Making in a Time of Plague."[105] Thus, the focus, as such, was on an epidemic situation.

The exercise again consisted of a moderated discussion round, in which the moderator read the current situation report on the spreading epidemic from a script. Participants were then asked to explain how they would behave in the corresponding situation and to discuss this with each other. The following level of escalation was debated:

"In several cities, shootings have occurred over the distribution of antibiotics. In most affected states, the National Guard has been called in to provide for the secure distribution of antibiotics and medical resources and to ensure the continued safety of hospital operations. The sight of an armed military presence in US cities has provoked protests about curtailment of civil liberties, but at the same time some governors are requesting additional support from the Department of Defense in the provision of supplies, personnel, and security.

"There is wide state-to-state variation in isolation policies and actions. In some states, any person with symptoms that could be plague is placed in mandatory isolation under guard. ... Each state is deciding whether to impose restrictions on public movement, including possible curfews, possible prohibition on meetings of more than a few people, and possible closure of highways, airports, and train stations."[106]

After the scenario was read out, a simulated telephone conference call followed in which the participants discussed whether this type of forced isolation and quarantine was a good idea or not. The discussion moderator, Tara O'Toole, who, at the time, was vice president of the Center for Civilian Biodefense Strategies and also the author of the script, instructed the group to "please have this conversation?"[107]

The role of the government's emergency management officer was played by Jerome Hauer, who, at the time—a year before the 9/11 attacks—held the same position in real life in New York City, where he headed the Office of Emergency Management. Hauer considered the following:

> "The question is, however, how do we enforce it and to what degree? How much force do you use to keep people in their homes? I'd certainly like to understand how we can go about it when we use the National Guard, because they haven't been federalized so we can use them along with our local police for law enforcement purposes."[108]

The group was then informed that, according to the script, Congress had just passed an emergency law that would allow the federal government to issue a quarantine directive to the states. The moderator turned to Margaret Hamburg, a senior official in the Department of Health and Human Services who played the US Secretary of Health and Human Services in the exercise. She suggested:

"I would recommend or put in place bans on public gatherings and recommend that people stay at home if they're not sick. I would make recommendations about various sorts of restrictions of travel, but I would not try to impose a true quarantine in the sort of classical sense."[109]

With hindsight, it becomes clear that important issues that are of concern to politicians and the public in the coronavirus crisis were already being discussed very seriously among a small group of people responsible for emergency management twenty years earlier. However, the simulation exercises from 1999 and 2000 were only the starting point for a whole series of similar exercises conducted by the Center that were subsequently further refined and filled with increasingly more high-level positions.

Looking at it today, it seems as if they had purposefully prepared for a state of emergency in connection with an epidemic, with such an event being imagined increasingly clearly, in ever more detail, so that all eventualities and all conceivable variants having been discussed so often and so intensively that, when threatened, and the danger finally became a reality, they could simply rewind the tape for the prepared plans.

Almost all the participants at these events belonged to a small biosecurity coterie, held various key positions in public agencies, consulting firms, and research institutions, and seamlessly alternated between state and private institutions. One encounters their names not only in the context of the exercises but also in important government positions: Tara O'Toole, Jerome Hauer, Margaret Hamburg, James Woolsey, Jeffrey Smith. Some of them had known each other for many years, some had intelligence connections. Jeffrey Smith, for example, who participated in several exercises, had been head attorney of the CIA. Tara O'Toole, who developed the scripts for some of the exercises and later joined the US Government as Under Secretary of Homeland Security for Science and Technology, subsequently became a Member of the Board of In-Q-Tel, a CIA company that invests in young, hi-tech companies whose products are of interest to the agency.[110]

The next simulation exercise (Dark Winter, June 2001) was once again significantly more professional. The meetings no longer took place at a hotel, but rather at the highly secure Andrews Air Force Base near Washington DC. The exercise again concerned a smallpox attack, which seemed to be something of an obsession of the authors. This time, according to the script, it began in Oklahoma. The state's governor, Frank Keating, took part in the exercise, playing himself.

The planners proudly reported that the participants included five well-known mainstream media journalists who were present at a simulated press conference, including the abovementioned *New York Times* reporter Judith Miller.[111] For the exercise, deceptively real-looking, "live" television news broadcasts on the bioweapons attack had been specially pre-produced for additional authenticity and thrill and were played to the participants via video interspersed with shocking images of people infected with smallpox.

Part of the exercise included the steady presentation of the statistics of the developing case numbers and curves that are now so familiar from the coronavirus crisis. According to the script, a type of lockdown (the word was not yet used at the time) was implemented. Public life was shut down and schools and borders were closed. The pros and cons of declaring martial law were also discussed.

But, above all, it was about vaccines. Were there enough? Was compulsory vaccination necessary? The planners were again concerned that unwanted information might spread uncontrollably.

In this context, it was asked whether laws might be needed "to prohibit dangerous information,"[112] since false information about the smallpox outbreak could surface on the Internet and might include false reports about remedies.[113]

At the end of the Dark Winter simulation exercise, which reckoned with one million deaths, the actor playing the US president, ex-Senator Sam Nunn, appeared before the simulated public and explained:

"We now believe that by using various private US pharmaceutical facilities we can be manufacturing about 12 million doses of smallpox vaccine per month. First dose will still not be available for 5 weeks. We must keep in mind that this will be an unlicensed vaccine that will not have been tested in humans."[114]

The enforced restrictions on freedom, according to the script, caused both serious economic and democratic damage. In a review, the authors formulated one of their core questions: "To what extent can and should the government infringe upon civil liberties? Under what conditions can those powers be exercised?"[115] The script itself stated:

"Americans can no longer take basic civil liberties such as freedom of assembly or travel for granted."[116]

What was striking in all these exercises was that it was not only a state-of-health crisis that was played out, with overburdened hospitals and epidemic deaths, but strangely, in all the scripts, riots always broke out so that it was necessary to respond to these with the use of the military and strong restrictions on freedoms and civil liberties. It seemed that the bioterror exercises, with their frequent smallpox and plague attack scenarios, also served as a pretext for a thorough rehearsal of a political state of emergency. Apparently, such an event was expected.

The Dark Winter exercise took place in June 2001, three months before the attacks of 9/11. After this, the danger posed by bioweapons once again came to the public's attention, triggered above all by the anthrax attacks at the time—attacks that to this day still raise many questions.

Letters containing the deadly powder reached, among others, two influential senators in September and October of 2001, at the same time that a legislative package with highly controversial content was being discussed in Congress. The USA PATRIOT Act (also known as the Patriot Act) made possible the detention of foreign terror suspects indefinitely without trial. In passing the Patriot Act, the government laid the groundwork for the Guantanamo system that has resulted in US secret prisons around the world.[117]

The radical legislative package also facilitated eavesdropping on US citizens and the domestic use of intelligence services inside the United States.[118]

Two influential critics of these changes were Senator Tom Daschle, Senate Majority Leader, and Senator Patrick Leahy, chairman of the Judiciary Committee.[119] Both had the institutional power to obstruct the legislative process, and both received threatening letters containing the deadly anthrax pathogens during exactly this time. The origin of these letters has not yet been discovered. Daschle and Leahy subsequently gave up their opposition and agreed to the legislative package.[120] A short time later, Daschle was asked by Vice President Cheney in a telephone call to not investigate the 9/11 attacks in a congressional commission in order to not withdraw any forces from the War on Terror.[121]

The official hypotheses of the government as to who was behind the anthrax attacks changed several times. They first suggested it was Osama Bin Laden and Al Qaeda, who would now, after the airplane attacks on the Twin Towers, allegedly carry out a "second wave" of attacks using bioterrorism. They then suggested it was Iraq. The fear spread by the media that Bin Laden or Saddam Hussein might strike with bioweapons was used by the government as an argument for their war plans against Afghanistan and Iraq.

But there was no evidence to support these hypotheses. From 2002 onwards, the investigative direction turned 180 degrees. Authorities began investigating a bioweapons researcher from their own military laboratory in Fort Detrick. However, this proved to be a false lead. The suspect, Steven Hatfill, successfully sued the US government for damages.

Beginning in 2008, it was suddenly reported that Bruce Ivins, another bioweapons researcher from the military laboratory in Fort Detrick, was responsible for the anthrax letters. Shortly after the investigation began, he committed suicide, which led to the termination of the trial. However, in 2010, during a hearing at the US National Academy of Sciences, it seemed to be evident that Ivins could not have been responsible for the anthrax attacks.[122] Suspicion of a conspiracy by government operatives has been in the air ever since.[123]

The abruptly deceased Ivins had explosive insider knowledge. In the 1990s, he had researched an anthrax vaccine, which, as mentioned in the previous chapter, was to be administered to more than two million US soldiers, the plan for which was later discontinued.[124] In 2000, the Pentagon commissioned Ivins and some of his colleagues to provide technical support to BioPort, a company which had failed to get an anthrax vaccine ready for approval.[125] The explosive information: One of the owners of the company, Admiral William Crowe, was previously Chairman of the Joint Chiefs of Staff, and thus the top US military official.[126] After the 9/11 attacks, official approval was rapidly given and everything ran like clockwork.[127]

4

Atlantic Storm: Epidemics as Door Openers (2001–2018)

After the 9/11 attacks, the subject of biosecurity literally exploded. This was also seen in the individual companies' stock exchange prices. Shares in the small pharmaceutical company Acambis rose by forty-five percent after the company struck a 400 million-dollar deal with the US government shortly after the collapse of the Twin Towers. In the deal, Acambis committed to the delivery of a smallpox vaccine that could be administered to the entire population in an emergency.[128]

As described above in the case of BioPort, it was also apparent in this instance that a relatively small company, which appeared to be far from economically stable, had been awarded this contract.[129] This company, too, had close ties to the government. The head of research at Acambis, Thomas Monath, was a retired US Army colonel, a former chief virologist at Fort Detrick, and the CIA's chief scientific adviser from 1998 to 2000.[130]

The contract had been awarded by the US Secretary of Health and Human Services, Tommy Thompson, for whose staff the risk of an attack by smallpox was so acute that these large sums were being spent on prevention (sums which were correspondingly lacking in other expenditures in the health sector) because the descriptions in the simulated scenarios over the previous months and years had repeatedly and specifically named smallpox. After 9/11, these scripts paid off immediately for some pharmaceutical companies.

Manufacturers in Europe also benefited. At the beginning of 2003, the German Federal Minister for Health, Ulla Schmidt, ordered a smallpox vaccine for many millions of euros without a bidding process. In an explanatory memo to the German Federal Ministry of Finance, she wrote that Germany was a "particularly attractive target for bioterrorist attacks" and there would be "about 25 million" dead after an attack with the smallpox virus. In view of the looming war in Iraq and due to the "acute aggravation of the risk situation," it would therefore be necessary to expediate the procurement. The security authorities allegedly had evidence that smallpox pathogens were being stored in Russia, Iraq, and North Korea. There would also be evidence that terrorists were trying to produce bioweapons. When her intergovernmental note became public, the minister backpedaled.[131] Three weeks before the start of the Iraq War, Angela Merkel, still leader of the opposition at the time, called in vain for a parliament debate on the terror threat of smallpox.[132] The German weekly news magazine *Der Spiegel*, wrote:

"It is debatable whether the smallpox vaccine that is no longer approved in Germany may be used for preventive vaccinations. 'There are emergency regulations that already exist and allow this,' explained RKI President Kurth. In addition, the federal government has agreed to take over insurance cover for phase one of the plan if any of those vaccinated are harmed by it."[133]

In total, the German federal government spent 200 million euros on the procurement of a smallpox vaccine during this period.[134]

Such questionable dealings were not new. What changed after September 11, 2001 was something more fundamental: The issue of biosecurity became purposefully institutionalized and internationalized. In other words, cross-border structures were established to synchronize national policy responses to an epidemic. The origins of today's global "coronavirus synchronization," i.e., the almost uniform reaction of various countries to the appearance of the virus, lie in this systematically promoted development.

It began shortly after 9/11 with a conference initiated by the abovementioned Tommy Thompson, the US Secretary of Health and Human Services. At his initiative, and justified by the anthrax attacks which were widely reported in the media, a meeting was held that included the health ministers of Germany, France, Italy, the UK, Canada, Japan, Mexico, and the US.[135] The participating countries were those comprising the G7 group of nations, with the additional inclusion of Mexico. Together they founded the so-called Global Health Security Initiative.

The announced goal was to "share information and coordinate efforts to improve global health security,"[136] referring mainly to bioweapon attacks. From the outset it was also about vaccines and common regulations for their purchase. Among other things, the ministers agreed to cooperate in the procurement of vaccines for the future, to conduct constructive dialogue on the legal framework for vaccine development, to exchange contingency plans between each other, to carry out joint exercises, and to better network high-security laboratories around the world.[137]

After this, by their own account, the group met annually as an informal circle, and thus no official decisions were made. However, precisely because the ministers (or their closest confidants) met in person, the meetings had national political impact. From the very beginning there was pressure:

"To urgently take this process forward, each of us [cabinet ministers] will designate a senior official to be the point person to ensure that this Plan is translated into concrete actions. Officials from each country will meet without delay to flesh out specific measures of this Plan. In addition, these senior officials constitute a network of rapid communication/reaction in case of crisis."[138]

This was written in the group's first document published in November 2001. A year later, in December 2002, the health ministers of the eight countries took the next far-reaching step. They expanded the program of coordinated emergency planning to include pandemics:

"We recognized that there are many commonalities in preparedness and response for bioterrorism and influenza pandemic. We agreed to establish a technical working group on influenza pandemic, which will be co-chaired by the US and the UK, to address existing gaps and research and development needs. This work should be carried out in conjunction with the WHO and other appropriate international organizations."[139]

Thus, the newly-created network for the synchronization of policies was therefore not only to be used in the event of a terrorist attack, but also in an epidemic that would occur across national boundaries.

One must keep in mind that the creation of the entire structure that decided on all these measures "informally" (but implemented them in very real terms), was based on a fallacy, namely on the claim that the anthrax attacks had been committed by a foreign terrorist group, which could also threaten other countries in a similar manner. With the resulting fear, the entire Western world, beginning in the US, was drawn into an exercise that was becoming increasingly complex. In all the scenarios, this led to three objectives: a state of emergency, mass vaccination, and extended state powers of intervention. This was what was being rehearsed.

The international group's first exercise took place from September 8 to September 10, 2003, under the name Global Mercury. Because of the SARS outbreak in the same year, the exercise had to be postponed. The attendees no longer met in one place but played out the scenario—another smallpox outbreak—simultaneously in all participating governmental agencies in the eight countries. Representatives of the WHO and the European Commission also took part. Several hundred civil servants from all over the world participated.

Germany had three teams from both the Federal Ministry of Health and the Robert Koch Institute (the German counterpart to the CDC), who alternated in eight-hour shifts.[140] Communication among the participants during the crisis was tested, which, as anticipated, did not proceed smoothly. The team around the exercise leader, who was hierarchically above the participants (see the following diagram), repeatedly fed so-called "injects" into the event—current news, e-mails or telephone calls—to which the participants, i.e., politicians and heads of government, had to react.

The participants came to the conclusion that in future crises there should be a central information hub that collected and distributed all data. This role was to be given to the WHO. [141]

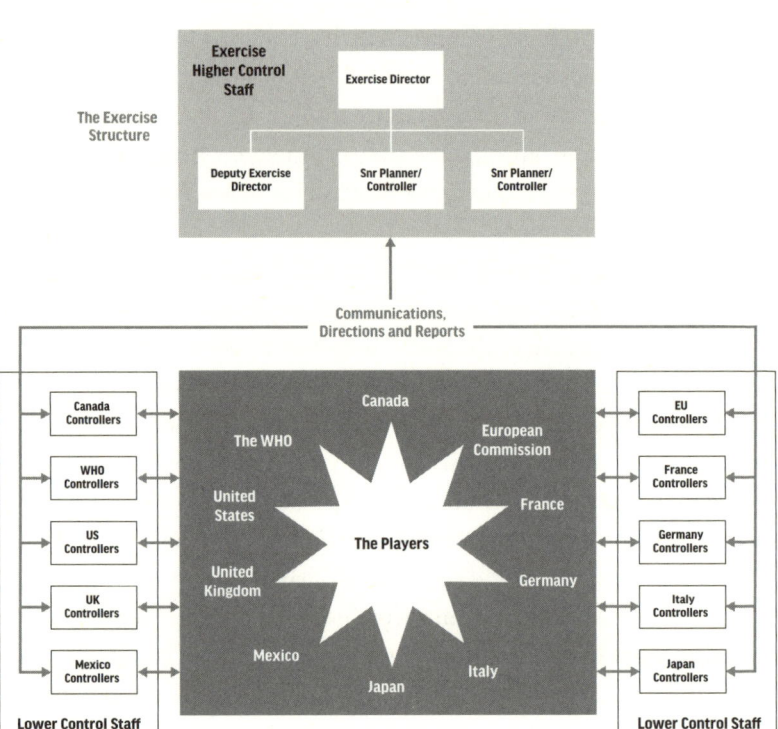

The main innovation of the exercise was its internationality. With the US, Japan, Germany, France, the UK, and other countries, some of the world's strongest economic powers were included as players in the planning.

This enormously increased complexity resulting from multinational coordination processes was further rehearsed. The professionals around Tara O'Toole from the Center for Civilian Biodefense Strategies, which had since been renamed the Center for Biosecurity, again took over this task. The center designed another exercise that was held in Washington on January 14, 2005, under the name Atlantic Storm. This tied in

The diagram caption reads: This diagram from the final report of the Global Mercury exercise, which took place in September 2003, shows the intended roles of the planners and co-players. 142

with exercise Dark Winter from 2001 and was now also internationalized. The main question was: "How would world leaders manage the catastrophe of a fast-moving global epidemic of deadly disease?"[143]

The exercise, which this time took place not at a military base, but at the newly-opened, five-star Mandarin Oriental hotel in Washington DC, was deemed so important that the organizers first practiced a trial run four days prior to the actual event with other participants.[144]

The cast for the exercise round was more high-level this time. The role of US president was played by former US Secretary of State Madeleine Albright and the head of the WHO was played by former Norwegian Prime Minister Gro Harlem Brundtland, who had also recently led the WHO in real life. The German chancellor was represented by Werner Hoyer, former Minister of State at the German Foreign Office and a reserve air force major. Hoyer later said:

"For someone who has been around in the security and defense fields in its traditional sense for many years, this was quite a surprising and breathtaking exercise. This is something I think a very small minority of politicians in Europe are aware of."[145]

In addition to the eleven players, including Hoyer, more than a hundred observers from politics, the military, the media, and the pharmaceutical industry were invited. Representatives from two vaccine manufacturers were present. In addition, among the German observers were Florian Reindel, a high-ranking employee of Wolfgang Ischinger, then the German ambassador in Washington; US correspondent for the *Frankfurter Allgemeine Zeitung*, Matthias Rüb; Thomas

Kleine-Brockhoff from the German weekly *Die Zeit* (later head of Federal President of Germany Joachim Gauck's planning department); and one representative from the Robert Koch Institute (RKI), Walter Biederbick, head of the RKI's Centre for Biological Threats and Special Pathogens and former Bundeswehr (German army) officer in NATO's operations planning department.[146]

Biederbick was also part of a fourteen-member Transatlantic Biosecurity Network, whose members, according to the organizers, had advised on the exercise "in a personal capacity and not as official representatives of their nations or employers."[147] Later, Biederbick contributed to research at the RKI on the topic of crisis communication in the event of a pandemic, which, in his words, should be "intensely coordinated at the international level," since it would be "disastrous if each country were to communicate something different."[148]

The international scene that came together in this exercise represented precisely the fusion of politics, pharmaceutical industry, scientific research, military, and media that the organizers wanted—all with a transatlantic imprint, meaning under US leadership.

Among the invited observers was also Anders Tegnell, the current Swedish chief epidemiologist, then project manager for the development of a pandemic plan for Sweden. Tegnell was, apparently, less easily integrated, and in any case famously went his own way later during the coronavirus crisis.

According to the scenario, the heads of state of the US, the UK, Canada, Germany, France, Italy, Sweden, the Netherlands, and Poland, as well as the heads of the European Commission and the WHO, had gathered for an unspecified "Transatlantic Security Summit" when they learned of a smallpox outbreak. The script described the following situation:

"On January 13, the eve of the summit, smallpox cases were reported in Germany, the Netherlands, Sweden, and Turkey. The leaders decide to meet for a few hours on the 14th before heading home to deal with the emerging crisis.

"During the six hour meeting, the transatlantic leaders wrestled with the enormity and rapid pace of the emerging epidemics of smallpox, the tension between domestic politics and international relations, the challenge of controlling the movement of people across borders, and an international shortage of critical medical resources such as smallpox vaccine.

"The total number of reported smallpox cases rose throughout the day from 51 cases in four European countries at 9:00 am to 3,320 cases throughout Europe and North America just 4.5 hours later at 1:30 pm—with projections indicating the possibility of 660,000 cases worldwide within 30 days. Ultimately, the outbreaks were discovered to be the result of covert attacks on transportation hubs and centers of commerce in six cities: Istanbul, Rotterdam, Warsaw, Frankfurt, New York, and Los Angeles."[149]

In a report in the German newspaper *Die Zeit*, the participating journalist, Thomas Kleine-Brockhoff, described what then happened:

"In no time at all, the summit became an operations center. Dramatic decisions had to be made: Quarantine? Close the borders? Begin with mass vaccinations? Distribute the vaccine across the world? Declare a military emergency? Or even the collective defense clause of NATO's founding treaty? More than three years after the attacks on New York and Washington, it remained to be seen whether those in power were better able to cope with the challenges of terror. The American president, Madeleine Albright, opened the crisis meeting with the appeal that it would 'hopefully be possible to act together.' As a confidence-building measure, she suggested: 'We should call each other by our first names. We are all friends here at the table.' … The players, all high-ranking veterans of transatlantic politics, were familiar with summits and crises. They were sitting in the ballroom of a luxury Washington hotel. Spotlights illuminated the conference table. Around the table, it was pitch dark. That is where the observers and extras were sitting."[150]

What was striking about the initial situation was that the heads of state became aware of the events at a time when they accidentally happened to be meeting at a summit, and therefore were able to easily coordinate with each other. The same thing actually happened in January 2020, when many political leaders learned of the coronavirus crisis when they met at the World Economic Forum in Davos (see Chapter 8).

As in Dark Winter, the exercise also included pre-produced television news broadcasts in order to ensure that events were more realistic for the players. These were shown on large screens "to give the group a sense of what their publics were seeing on television."[151] At a staged press conference that was part of the exercise, the invited journalists also became active players in the exercise and could rehearse dialogues with the politicians that might be expected in the event of a crisis.

Among the questions discussed during the exercise was the following, which seems explosive in view of the current coronavirus crisis:

"How should national leaders determine the risks and/
or benefits of various disease control measures such as
border closure or quarantine? Under what conditions
would the significant economic, political, and social consequences of such actions might [sic] be outweighed by
the potential benefits? If actions are taken to restrict the
movement of people, for how long would restrictions
have to be maintained, how would they be coordinated
internationally, and how would the decision be made to
lift them?"[152]

The deeper question lurking beneath all these considerations was what would trigger a state of emergency in which
essential freedoms could be overridden. Where was the start
button of this machine? Although the creators of Atlantic Storm imagined a terrorist attack, the evaluation report
emphasized several times that all preparations and plans would
apply equally to "a naturally occurring pandemic of infectious
disease." At one point, in this context, there was literally talk
of a "future SARS."[153]

In 2005, when this exercise took place, the focus of the biosecurity community began to shift more and more from terrorist
attacks to pandemics, especially with the appearance of avian
influenza in the same year, which led to a media storm of agitation that is, in some ways, reminiscent of today's coronavirus anxiety. The disease, which, according to WHO figures in
2005 and 2006, resulted in only 122 deaths worldwide,[154] was
declared a global threat by the US government and portrayed
as such by many media outlets at the time.

Against this background, US President George W. Bush presented a comprehensive plan in a press conference on November 1, 2005 to help protect the country from an impending

influenza pandemic. Also present was the WHO's director-general, who had been specially flown in from Geneva. "Scientists and doctors cannot tell us where or when the next pandemic will strike or how severe it will be," Bush said, "but most agree: at some point, we are likely to face another pandemic." People around the globe were therefore in urgent need of protection. He went on in giant rhetorical steps: "Because a pandemic could strike at any time, we can't waste time in preparing. So to meet all our goals, I'm requesting a total of \$7.1 billion in emergency funding from the United States Congress."[155] Most of this money was intended for vaccines, including Tamiflu developed by Gilead Sciences, which had been run by Bush's secretary of defense, Donald Rumsfeld, until 2001. Rumsfeld still owned shares in the pharmaceutical company worth millions of dollars in 2005, and thus also benefited privately from the government's scaremongering.[156]

Among others, the WHO was on board in the person of Klaus Stöhr, head of the organization's influenza program. For months, Stöhr repeatedly warned against avian influenza in an alarmist tone and was regularly cited in the media as a supposedly independent expert: The disease would have an "unprecedented dimension" that had "never been seen before in history."[157] In the autumn of 2005, Stöhr predicted a spreading of avian influenza in Germany and complained that governments were still not spending enough money on vaccines. Avian influenza, according to the WHO epidemiologist, "is a candidate that could probably cause the next pandemic."[158] Two years later, after the avian flu hype had passed and governments around the world, at the recommendation of the WHO,[159] had bought billions of dollars' worth of vaccines—the effectiveness of which soon turned out to be dubious[160]—Stöhr left the WHO and joined the pharmaceutical company Novartis.

The doctor and former politician Wolfgang Wodarg, who was widely reviled in the coronavirus crisis in 2020, stated in January 2006, as a member of the German parliament:

> "Avian influenza is not at all a human disease; we are talking about a phantom. It is only a theory that a disease that occurs in birds can be dangerous to humans. Animal diseases that become dangerous to humans are dependent on the number of pathogens, i.e., the intensity of the contact, and … the immunity status of those who are normally able to withstand contact with these pathogens. If these are in disproportion, you could become ill. But this has been known in medicine for thousands of years. Living in close contact with animals if the immune system is weakened, that is dangerous. In such cases, other diseases, all of which I cannot list, can also infect humans.
>
> "In countries in which no cases of Avian influenza—I am using the term this one time—have been discovered, these are often countries where there is no money for the corresponding tests because the emphasis there is on much different problems.
>
> "I have asked myself how it has actually happened that we are talking so much about this issue. Who has an interest in bringing this issue to the fore? For the media, this subject is welcome. But it would also take up another subject if that frightened people. The media likes to do that. But there are also other profiteers, namely those who sell Tamiflu and issue the licenses. I highly recommend that you find out who owns stock shares, who has exerted pressure, what processes have already been carried out and what strategies are being used to sell as

much of the stuff as possible. We cannot simply dismiss these questions, for these are the engines of fear. They serve to frighten people, unnecessarily."[161]

Wodarg raised questions that have resurfaced in the coronavirus crisis: What role does virus testing play? Does mass testing for tiny viral genetic snippets only create the perception of a crisis? How meaningful are the results when relatively few people die at the same time (which was the case with avian influenza)? Finally, is the virus itself life-threatening, or will it only become so when immune systems are weakened—which could also have economic and social causes? Why is the focus on the single virus as a "human killer" and not on the environment in which it can spread, i.e., poor living conditions, poverty, lack of hygiene, and so on? These issues have been—and still are—seldom discussed. Instead, attention is focused on vaccines.

The same game was repeated in 2009 with the swine flu, also called "new influenza." In total, in Germany alone, the federal government and the states spent 330 million euros on Tamiflu and other medications that, for the most part, were never used and had to be destroyed after their expiration date.[162]

The economic interests of the pharmaceutical industry remained an important driving force of public attention around the issue of pandemics. Tara O'Toole, director of the Center for Biosecurity and the scriptwriter of many of the exercises mentioned above, was also personally involved in this structure. As her career progressed and US President Barack Obama appointed her Under Secretary of Homeland Security for Science in 2009, it became public that, in her nomination process, she had concealed work as an adviser to a lobbying organization funded by the pharmaceutical industry. O'Toole had signed letters from this group called the Alliance for Biosecurity, calling on Congress and government agencies to spend more money on vaccines.[163]

The lobby group itself was not registered as such and had no own office and no account, but was managed through the law firm Drinker Biddle,[164] whose Washington head, Anita Cicero, organized and represented a number of interest groups in the pharmaceutical industry on several occasions and was in regular contact with US Congress representatives, the WHO, the European Commission, and other senior officials.[165] In 2010, she became deputy director of the Center for Biosecurity, formerly headed by O'Toole, and which currently plays an important role in the coronavirus crisis.

After moving from the law firm servicing the pharmaceutical industry, where she was responsible for more than 300 attorneys and other employees, to the "independent and non-profit" Center for Biosecurity, Cicero launched several initiatives that led to the further internationalization of pandemic emergency planning. For example, she started a number of initiatives for the improvement of mutual understanding and cooperation between US and Chinese scientists and public health officials working in the field of epidemic preparedness,[166] as well as similar cooperation programs with Saudi Arabia, Kuwait, India, Thailand, and Indonesia. Was Cicero only concerned with global health security? Or was she perhaps also concerned with the interests of those companies seeking to expand their markets that she had represented as a lawyer for more than a decade?

The political potential of pandemics was finally highlighted in a study by The Rockefeller Foundation published in the spring of 2010. It presented four conceivable future global scenarios, one of which, referred to as Lockstep, depicted an authoritarian world full of state surveillance and coercion, which, according to the authors, would prevail around the globe after a major influenza pandemic and the ensuing global financial crisis.[167]

The model resembles the year 2020 in an astonishing number of ways. It explicitly describes how China, in the course of the fictitious pandemic, with its particularly authoritarian protective measures, would become a model to the world. The authors also mention the mandatory use of face-masks in many countries, and further remarked that "even after the pandemic faded, this more authoritarian control and oversight of citizens and their activities stuck and even intensified."[168] The editors, in their own words, said they wanted to "seed a new strategic conversation among the key public, private, and philanthropic stakeholders."[169] For the German journalist Norbert Häring, the document shows that "for at least the past ten years, important players have been thinking about the political and social possibilities and challenges that are created by fear-inducing pandemics."[170]

There is further evidence of these kinds of ideas in elite circles. Jacques Attali, a leading thinker of the French elite, longtime adviser to French President François Mitterand, and "discoverer" of Emmanuel Macron,[171] philosophized openly in May 2009 at the beginning of the media hype regarding swine flu:

"History teaches us that humanity only evolves significantly if it is truly frightened ... The incipient pandemic could trigger one of these structured fears. ... A major pandemic [if severe, author's addition] will be able to raise awareness of the need for altruism better than any humanitarian ecological discourse ... And even in this crisis, which we of course have to hope is not very serious, we must not forget, as we did in the financial crisis, to learn from it—so that prevention and control mechanisms and logistical processes for the fair distribution of medicines and vaccines can be set up before the next inevitable crisis. To this end, we must establish a global policy, global storage, and, with that, global taxation. Then we will be able to lay the foundations for a genuine global government much faster than it would have been possible for economic reasons alone."[172]

The worldwide networking of emergency planning and the related exercise activities moved forward simultaneously in great strides. In May 2012, the Center for Biosecurity organized a conference with the title "Improving Epidemic Response: Building Bridges Between the US and China."[173] The opening speech was given by the eighty-seven-year-old General Brent Scowcroft, a close confidant of Henry Kissinger and himself national security adviser to several US presidents. Scowcroft had been part of the team that had discreetly prepared for the resumption of diplomatic relations between communist China and the US in 1972, after more than twenty years of silence between the two powers. He now also welcomed close cooperation with the Chinese in the field of biosecurity.

At the conference, the US and Chinese reported on their growing relations in this field, in particular on pandemic contingency planning. They had already been working together for several years in a close network. The US Centers for Disease Control (CDC) had an office with about fifty employees in Beijing at the time (in 2020 there were only fourteen), from where this cooperation was coordinated.[174] The US also managed a training program for Chinese epidemiologists and it was proudly noted that seventy of the graduates were now in executive positions in Chinese healthcare agencies.[175]

They also helped bring US pharmaceutical companies like Pfizer into contact with Chinese researchers.[176] The work of the Americans was complex and went as far as training and teaching public relations methods, according to a CDC report:

> "Activities included offering training workshops on media communication, conducting press interviews, and arranging for a three-week training in the fall, with the U.S. CDC headquarters immunization communication staff. During this training, communications specialists from the Chinese immunization program will learn how U.S. communication specialists respond to anti-vaccine sentiment in the United States and how to effectively communicate with the public during crises."[177]

An effective public relations strategy was also a major focus of the work of the Center for Biosecurity, which was renamed the Center for Health Security in 2013. The name change could also be interpreted as an expression of the intended fusion of health and security policy.

The center's work culminated in two major exercises that immediately preceded the coronavirus crisis: Clade X in May 2018, and Event 201 in October 2019. While the first rehearsed the US government's national response to a pandemic, the second played out an international response involving private corporations. Two months later, the coronavirus emerged.

5

Clade X: A Bioweapon for Population Reduction (2018)

After increasingly apocalyptic pandemic exercises were staged in rapid staccato in the years 1998 to 2005, shaped by the context of the War on Terror, the intensity subsequently subsided. Little happened for more than ten years. The major global financial crisis apparently offered few points of reference for smallpox exercises after 2008 and the 2009 swine flu fiasco[178] had first to be digested.

The situation changed with the emergence of Donald Trump, an event that was symbolic of the visible decline of the US-led global system. Shortly after his election as US president in November 2016, which at first seemed unbelievable to many observers and sent shockwaves around the globe, the exercises began anew.

Simultaneously, Bill Gates' efforts to link the issues of vaccines, international security, and bioterrorism intensified. In January 2017, he traveled to Davos for the World Economic Forum, where he said there needed to be "serious discussions about what the preparation should be for a possible attack with biological weapons."[179] Gates announced that he wanted to explore this issue in greater depth at the Munich Security Conference in February of that year. The reason for this was the launch of CEPI (Coalition for Epidemic Preparedness Innovations),[180] a vaccine research initiative that he co-founded with the pharmaceutical industry and several governments. This was aimed at developing vaccines much more rapidly than before—in less than twelve months, rather than within ten years—and securing public-private funding.[181]

The Munich Security Conference, which Gates subsequently attended, was fully in the shadow of Donald Trump's move to the White House in 2017. The German newspaper *Frankfurter Allgemeine Zeitung (FAZ)* reported a "peculiar atmosphere in the corridors and back rooms" of the conference venue:

"Rarely—perhaps never before—have the faces of the newly arrived heads of state, ministers, advisers, and experts been so marked with questions. Growing uncertainty, insecurity, and distrust preoccupied the participants and overshadowed all the discussions: Will America abandon Europe? Is NATO fragmenting? And, above all, what will hold the West together in the future? … It is as if more than 20 heads of state, more than 80 ministers, consultants, and experts—in short, the elite of foreign and security policy-makers—have come together for what is probably the largest group therapy session this organization has experienced in this century. With one uncertain goal: to find out what common ground remains, and whether it still supports a Western security architecture."[182]

John McCain, one of the most influential foreign policy experts in the US, hit "the core of the Western crisis of the soul" in his speech. The question as to whether the West would survive, McCain said, had previously been dismissed as alarmism, but was now "dead serious." The conservative hardliner (who died a year later) concluded his speech, which received thunderous applause from the assembled audience of world leaders and military officers with the pithy confession: "I refuse to accept the demise of our world order."[183]

At the same conference, in front of the same audience, Bill Gates gave his speech the following day. In it he explained the dangers and possible details of a major pandemic:

> "It's also true that the next epidemic could originate on the computer screen of a terrorist intent on using genetic engineering to create a synthetic version of the smallpox virus ... or a super contagious and deadly strain of the flu. ... Whether it occurs by a quirk of nature or at the hand of a terrorist, epidemiologists say a fast-moving airborne pathogen could kill more than 30 million people in less than a year. ... We need to ... prepare for epidemics the way the military prepares for war. This includes germ games and other preparedness exercises so we can better understand how diseases will spread, how people will respond in a panic, and how to deal with things like overloaded highways and communications systems."[184]

Three months later, for the first time in many years, the Johns Hopkins Center for Health Security began planning a new pandemic exercise, even larger and more complex than the previous ones. It was called Clade X. Preparations began in May 2017, four months after Trump entered the White House.[185]

This time the scenario was different. No smallpox, no plague, no anthrax, but rather a novel viral mix, developed, according to the script, in the laboratory of a biotech company; a genetic combination of a highly contagious parainfluenza virus and the particularly deadly Nipah virus. (The Nipah virus, incidentally, broke out in India at the same time as the actual exercise, and was contained there with the help of a researcher from

the US military who had developed a vaccine whose manufacturers received twenty-five million dollars in funding after
the outbreak.[186]

What was new about the exercise script was not only the
type of virus, but also the fact that the terrorists were no longer
assumed to be nameless and without biography, but that a background document of the drill described in surprising detail the
history of the fictitious terrorist group called ABD ("A Brighter
Dawn"). It stated:

"A Brighter Dawn was established in the 1990s in the United
States. The group's stated purpose was to slow and eventually reverse the degradation of the planet that was occurring from overpopulation. ABD's goal at that time was
to help humanity return to an earlier state of being. The
group's activities were uniformly peaceful at that time
and included lecture and discussion sessions, grassroots
activism, and outreach.

"By 2010, A Brighter Dawn's membership had grown sub-
stantially in both numbers and geographic diversity. There
were members and local chapters in many countries. At
around that time, a split appears to have occurred within A
Brighter Dawn. An extreme faction in ABD felt that direct
action was needed to achieve the 'reset' or 'paradigm shift'
that would be required to fundamentally alter the balance.

"This splinter group consisted of no more than 30 individuals. A charismatic leader assumed leadership, and he
worked closely with about 25 other ABD members in the
group who had bioscience training, including virologists.
Following the schism, the splinter group established a laboratory near Zurich, Switzerland, and masqueraded as a
small biotech start-up firm. They set up a sophisticated

life science laboratory with commercially available equipment and focused on developing a biological weapon that would have a global impact. ABD's leadership also seems to have been attracted to the concept of a biblical plague as the corrective to humanity's excesses. The splinter group's funding came from members, like-minded private donors, and involvement in illicit activities. ...

"Once the Clade X pathogen had been successfully developed and manufactured, volunteer ABD members, who were willing to risk being infected, traveled the globe with small volumes of liquid agent, which they disseminated using commercially available aerosolizers in crowded public places. The multiple attacks were relatively inefficient in that almost half the attacks failed to infect anyone; in the other attacks, only 50 people on average became clinically ill. But this was sufficient to touch off the Clade X pandemic."[187]

The exercise took place on May 15, 2018, in Washington DC, again at the luxury Mandarin Oriental hotel. The rehearsed outbreak began in Germany. A series of meetings of the US National Security Council were acted out where the players were again high-ranking US politicians, some of whom had already held similar or the same government and parliament functions in reality.[188]

One of the first events after the outbreak, according to the script, was the development of a PCR test to detect the virus.[189] The debate then revolved largely around travel restrictions and lockdowns (still called quarantine at the time). The "level of force authorized to maintain quarantine"[190] was discussed. It was concluded that more "legal clarity" would be needed on questions of "transfer of authority during quarantine." The government should also plan for "potential adverse consequences" of this type of quarantine, "including potential public resistance."[191]

In the exercise, the crisis was played out in fast motion. The outbreak to be regulated covered a period of many months. According to the scenario, the numbers of infected continued increasing and the death toll ended up at 150 million worldwide, of which fifteen million were in the US. According to the authors, these were still low numbers, made possible only by the fact that vaccine production was extremely accelerated.

At the end of the exercise, the first priority was thus to call on governments to immediately provide the necessary funding to be able to develop new vaccines "within months not years."[192] In particular, new mRNA vaccines were mentioned (as advocated for and funded by Bill Gates), which are based on genetic engineering, and which have played a major role in the current coronavirus crisis.[193] The recommendations of the planners of the exercise to the government stated:

"Recent developments in synthetic biology … are yielding new possibilities for rapid discovery of effective drugs and vaccines. Similarly, novel countermeasure approaches, like self-amplifying mRNA vaccines … have promise as platforms to enable quick development in an emergency. … This could all be done in a distributed way, allowing more people in more places to produce and scale production of countermeasures."[194]

On the whole, the event was considered a success by the organizers. Afterwards, they concluded that the exercise had reached a large public and raised awareness of the effects of pandemics.

The *Washington Post* wrote about the exercise three times. The message had also gotten through to experts and politicians: "Clade X has led to a series of follow-on presentations and events with the US Congress, the Biological Weapons Convention Meeting of Experts, the CDC, the Aspen Institute, and other organizations."[195] So, on several levels, the topic was back on the agenda.

Who funded the exercise? The organizers had been able to secure the support of the thirty-three-year-old Facebook cofounder Dustin Moskovitz and his Open Philanthropy Project as their chief sponsor. Moskovitz, one of the world's youngest self-made billionaires, wanted, in his own words, "to do as much good" as he could[196] with his wealth. Pandemics were, in the opinion of his foundation, "one of the biggest current risks to global welfare and stability," but research on pandemics had "relatively little" support thus far from private foundations, which was why the Open Philanthropy Project would fund the Johns Hopkins Center for Health Security.[197]

Here, too, there was no apparent ill will, only the best intentions. In a similar way, Moskovitz had already invested twenty million dollars in the US presidential campaign in September 2016 to prevent a last-minute Donald Trump victory.[198] The US would otherwise become isolated from the international community. Trump's campaign promises would be "quite possibly a deliberate con," while Hillary Clinton would represent a "vision of optimism, pragmatism, inclusiveness and mutual benefit."[199]

One could consider such statements from the young billionaire naïve and his intervention presumptuous, but ultimately such assessments do not matter. What is crucial is that people with such great wealth can, and do, use their influence. Moskovitz recognized this when, in a fit of near-schizophrenia, he said that he had "reservations about anyone using large amounts of money to influence elections." Yet, he would have to act this way in order "to do as much good" as he could.[200]

This "good" included the relaunch of the great pandemic machine, intended as a preventive measure to protect human lives. And the fact that the agenda behind it was significantly more complex, was apparently not only hidden from Moskovitz.

6

Event 201: Coronavirus Crisis as a Simulation Game (2019)

Meanwhile, word on the concept of Clade X had spread among the rich and influential. When the team from the Johns Hopkins Center for Health Security subsequently formulated an even larger, more complex follow-up exercise, the top league of sponsors came on board: the Bill and Melinda Gates Foundation and the World Economic Forum (WEF).

The WEF, known for its annual conference in the noble Swiss resort of Davos is, in its own words, a union of the world's 1,000 largest corporations "to shape a better future."[201] To this end, they aim to bring corporate leaders and heads of state together into continuous dialogue, supposedly pursuing no "ideological or commercial interests."[202]

At the heart of the organization are the Strategic Partners, around one hundred corporations that are particularly influential and who jointly control the orientation, goals and programs of the WEF. The Strategic Partners include, for example, Allianz, BlackRock, BP, Deutsche Bank, Facebook, the Bill and Melinda Gates Foundation, Goldman Sachs, Google, the pharmaceutical group Johnson & Johnson, Mastercard, PayPal, the oil corporation Saudi Aramco, Siemens, and the media group Thomson Reuters, owners of the Reuters news agency.[203]

The WEF could be described as a kind of modern "politburo of capitalism," where broad approaches to future international actions are considered and then jointly implemented. The common thread is an effort to globally integrate government and corporate interests, politely referred to as "public-private cooperation."

Thus, the WEF and the Bill and Melinda Gates Foundation were now financing the next major pandemic exercises together. This exercise had a fundamentally different approach than the previous ones—this time it was not a matter of rehearsing debates and votes within the government, but a strategy of cooperation between governments and global corporations during a pandemic. This is the description from the Johns Hopkins Center for Health Security:

"In recent years, the world has seen a growing number of epidemic events, amounting to approximately 200 events annually. These events are increasing, and they are disruptive to health, economies, and society. Managing these events already strains global capacity, even absent a pandemic threat. Experts agree that it is only a matter of time before one of these epidemics becomes global—a pandemic with potentially catastrophic consequences. A severe pandemic, which becomes 'Event 201,' would require reliable cooperation among several industries, national governments, and key international institutions. ... Similar to the Center's 3 previous exercises—Clade X, Dark Winter, and Atlantic Storm—Event 201 aimed to educate senior leaders at the highest level of US and international governments and leaders in global industries."[204]

Event 201 took place on October 18, 2019, two months before the appearance of the coronavirus, and also, rather disconcertingly, simulated the outbreak of a global coronavirus pandemic:

"Event 201 simulates an outbreak of a novel zoonotic [a disease that is transmissible from animals to humans] coronavirus transmitted from bats to pigs to people that eventually becomes efficiently transmissible from person to person, leading to a severe pandemic. The pathogen and the disease it causes are modeled largely on SARS, but it is more transmissible in the community setting by people with mild symptoms. ... There is no possibility of a vaccine being available in the first year. ... The scenario ends at the 18-month point, with 65 million deaths. The pandemic is beginning to slow due to the decreasing number of susceptible people. The pandemic will continue at some rate until there is an effective vaccine or until 80–90 % of the global population has been exposed. From that point on, it is likely to be an endemic childhood disease."[205]

Unlike in the previous exercises, there was no terrorist background—at least, there was no mention of it—and there was no longer talk of a sophisticated bioweapon, as was the case with Clade X the year before. This time, the pandemic was to have been simply a freak of nature.

And something else was specific to this simulation: The organizers and the players did not meet in Washington, the city of the government and governmental agencies, as in the previous events. Instead, they met in the center of the financial industry, in Manhattan, in the legendary luxury hotel The Pierre, once owned by J. Paul Getty, the richest man in the world, and exclusively located on Central Park. In The Pierre, where the bellboys still wear tails and top hats and where there are elevator operators as in the past, it was not only politicians and civil servants who met, but, for the most part, executives from global corporations. The executives were from the top management of their respective companies and those who were tasked with regulating international procedures within their corporations in the event of a major crisis. They therefore played themselves in the exercise rather than taking on other roles, which was also new. The fifteen players in the exercises included:[206]

Adrian Thomas, vice president of Johnson & Johnson, the largest pharmaceutical corporation in the world by market value and total turnover.

Jane Halton, former Minister of Health and Finance in Australia and longtime senior executive at the WHO, as well as chair of the Coalition for Epidemic Preparedness Innovations (CEPI), a "partnership" of the pharmaceutical industry, governments, and the WHO, which also plays a key role in the current coronavirus pandemic.

Matthew Harrington, global president and CEO of Edelman, the world's largest public relations agency, a "specialist in corporate positioning and reputation management with experience in crisis communications," and a personal advisor to Microsoft.[207] Hasti Taghi, vice president of NBC Universal, the world's third-largest media company.

Avril Haines, deputy director of the CIA and Deputy National Security Advisor under President Obama; later at a Washington lobbying firm that connects interested IT companies with the Pentagon and the intelligence agencies.[208] (Haines has been the Director of National Intelligence in the Biden Administration since January 2021).

These global managers were joined by the chairman of a medical products group, Lufthansa's chief crisis manager, the risk manager of the global Marriott International chain, the president of The UPS Foundation, and a representative of Singapore's central bank, the Monetary Authority of Singapore. Three other participants could be described as "pandemic professionals":

→ **Stephen Redd**, Deputy Director for Public Health and Implementation Service at the CDC, involved in the anthrax investigation after 9/11 and chief crisis manager in the 2009 swine flu fake[209] where he contributed to the vaccination of eighty-one million people in the US.[210]

→ **George Gao**, Director of the Chinese Center for Disease Control and Prevention, a virologist and avian influenza researcher, who, in January 2020, informed[211] the CDC head, Robert Redfield, about the danger of the coronavirus and, also in January 2020, co-wrote two of the first authoritative scientific articles on the coronavirus in professional Western periodicals.[212]

→ **Michael Ryan** (not personally present, but who gave his talk through a video connection), executive director of the WHO Health Emergencies Program since 2019 and, since 2020, the WHO's head crisis manager for COVID-19.

Event 201 gathered together many highly competent people, some of whom were to play an important role in the coronavirus crisis a few months later. The essence of both the exercise and the real-life situation that followed was a specific fusion of the themes of fear, widespread death, a state of emergency, administrative overload, restrictions of freedom, vaccines, regulation of pharmaceuticals, and media strategy. Specifically, a health emergency led to a global need for vaccines, for which corporations had to be given a more active role in international politics in order to finance, develop and distribute them, countering any resistance from the population with the help of PR strategies and the media. That was what the exercise was all about, and that is what it is all about today.

However, it is important to understand that it is not logical to deduce from these connections that the organizers and participants in the exercise "knew" about the impending real pandemic, which in turn would presuppose that the coronavirus crisis was deliberately planned and that the events were thus not a whim of nature, but a cover-up for the targeted use of a bioweapon. However, the astonishing similarity between practice and reality requires a closer look at how the actual 2020 pandemic began (see Chapter 8).

The organizers were aware of such speculation. According to the practice script, "conspiracy theories" appeared from the beginning of the fictional crisis, according to which "the pharmaceutical industry released this [virus]," which was why it was important to ensure "trust in pharmaceuticals and governments" in response to the emergency. Communication with the public in the crisis would need to be carefully planned.[213]

This issue was taken so seriously that a separate discussion about it took place during the exercise (Segment 4, Communications Discussion).[214] The vice president of NBC Universal emphasized that it was necessary to ensure that "the right representatives" would appear in the mainstream media in order to disseminate "our side of the story."[215] The former deputy director of the CIA added that the public arena should be "flooded" with their own arguments in order to reinforce the message.[216] The head of the public relations agency Edelman also pointed out that a centralized approach to the communication strategy should be taken and that a centrally-formulated message should then be made public through "informed advocates," appropriate representatives of NGOs and medical professionals. This centralization should also be international, which would require a database of facts and "key messages" to be disseminated worldwide.[217]

But it wasn't just about fact finding. The chairwoman of Bill Gates' vaccine development organization, CEPI, explained that it was not enough to merely disseminate facts and knowledge to the public in view of the virus. Rather, one should actively "incentivize the kind of behaviours we want to see."[218]

Following the exercise, recommendations were published. They called for closer cooperation between corporations and governments, the further expansion of an international vaccine reserve, the reduction of vaccine development regulations and an increased fight against disinformation:

> "Governments will need to partner with traditional and social media companies to research and develop nimble approaches to countering misinformation. This will require developing the ability to flood media with fast, accurate, and consistent information. ... National public health agencies should work in close collaboration with WHO to create the capability to rapidly develop and release consistent health messages. For their part, media companies should commit to ensuring that authoritative messages are prioritized and that false messages are suppressed including though the use of technology."[219]

The more than three-hour long discussions between the participants were released by the organizers shortly after the exercise, in full length as an Internet video.[220] Watching this material, one hardly has the impression of a meeting attended by malicious conspirators thirsting for action. The participants are more reminiscent of pale bureaucrats who perform the tasks assigned to the best of their ability. The debaters' desks are set up in U-shape, with the moderator at the front. To the left and right of the moderator are three previously unmentioned participants, who seem more knowledgeable and experienced than the others in both their appearance and speeches. Research shows that these three participants have something special in common that separates them from the other guests, and which also seems to have nothing to do with the topic of the exercise: All three have been closely linked to the topic of population control in their work for many years. They are:

→ **Christopher Elias**, president of Global Development at the Bill and Melinda Gates Foundation, whose responsibilities include family planning and vaccine delivery; also co-chair of Family Planning 2020, an international organization that is strongly committed to reducing the birthrate in selected countries (including India, Pakistan, Indonesia and large parts of Africa) and which promotes the large-scale use of contraception.

→ **Sofia Borges**, a member of the steering committee (the so-called Reference Group) of Family Planning 2020 and vice president of the UN Foundation, founded by billionaire Ted Turner, who advocates for a reduction of the global population by suggesting that "fertility rights could be sold so that poor people could profit from their decision not to reproduce."[221]

→ **Timothy Grant Evans**, co-founder of Gavi, The Vaccine Alliance, formerly a member of the Rockefeller Foundation, a member of the WHO Executive Board from 2003 to 2010 and Senior Director of Health, Nutrition and Population Global Practice at the World Bank from 2013 to 2019.

What is this all about? What does "population global practice" mean? And how are these issues linked to planning for a pandemic?

7

Excursus: Population Control

There is a fine line between helping the poor and steering or controlling them. The particularly wealthy have always seen it as their mission to develop plans for everyone else, especially for "Third World" countries. There are many problems with this, beginning with a lack of democratic legitimacy of the planners. Such programs become particularly problematic and worthy of criticism when the officially stated goals—aid and education for the poor—are superimposed onto other aspirations, such as influence and control.

Friendly and vague-sounding terms like "population global practice" or "family planning" often have the controversial goal of population control, which has been pursued very persistently by a network of international organizations over many years. The goal is that the world's population, especially in Africa, Asia, and Latin America, be reduced. This is justified by better development opportunities for these countries that would arise if there were fewer children to be provided for. A website published by the World Bank's department for Population Global Practice states:

> "Fertility is also a key driver of population dynamics. Many countries that are experiencing rapid population growth also have young populations. Such countries have the potential of benefiting from the demographic dividend: by investing in the health and well-being of their people

to build human capital, countries can reduce poverty and boost inclusive growth."[222]

These World Bank public relations formulations require translation since the language used conceals more than it is explains. "Demographic dividend" is public relations terminology. There is a dedicated website, "Demographic Dividend, Investing in Human Capital," created by the Bill & Melinda Gates Institute for Population and Reproductive Health at the Johns Hopkins Bloomberg School of Public Health, which states:

> "A demographic dividend is the accelerated economic growth that can result from improved reproductive health, a rapid decline in fertility, and the subsequent shift in population age structure. With fewer births each year, a country's working-age population grows larger relative to the young dependent population. With more people in the labor force and fewer children to support, a country has a window of opportunity for economic growth if the right social and economic investments and policies are made in health, education, governance, and the economy."[223]

This policy leads to a situation in the not-too-distant future in which the entire social burden is shifted to the shoulders of the few future adults, which then paralyzes society as a whole. This is advertised to the poorer countries as a liberation for women, who can finally decide for themselves whether they want children and, if so, how many. In addition, with fewer children, a larger proportion would survive and could be better educated and trained. Furthermore, there would be greater chances of finding a job in the future since there would also be less competition for jobs in a population that is decreasing in number. In order to achieve all of this, it would be necessary to provide easily accessible contraceptives. In this way, countries could "reap these dividends," as stated in an advertising document of the World Bank.[224]

What is not taken into account in this argument are the structural causes of poverty that are grounded in the international economic order. In this respect, however, according to these fine-sounding programs nothing is supposed to change. Instead, the impression is given that the order and rules of the world economy are, in themselves, fair, that poor countries simply have to use their opportunities wisely and ensure that their own citizens do not reproduce "unnecessarily," which would result in increased prosperity. The sociologist Shalini Randeria takes a critical view of this:

"I am disturbed by Western double standards. When a woman from Cameroon gives birth to several children, she allegedly contributes to global overpopulation, but when a Swiss person buys two cars, he boosts economic growth. The question of supposed overpopulation cannot be separated from resource consumption. The inhabitants of the city of New York consume more energy in one day than the entire African continent. If environmental protection is really important, it would be necessary to reduce the use of resources in industrialized countries, rather than worrying about the family size of foreign women in distant lands. ... It is always the others who are superfluous: the poor, the foreigners, the members of other religious communities. ... It is never just a question of numbers, but always about who is allowed to multiply and who is not."[225]

The findings of economists and experts like Joseph Stiglitz,[226] Naomi Klein,[227] Jean Ziegler,[228] John Pilger,[229] or Michel Chossudovsky,[230] which demonstrate that the global economic model promoted by Western countries creates neocolonial structures of dependence from which poor countries cannot alone free themselves, have been known for many years, but remain ignored.

Is concern for the well-being of the poor therefore really the main motive for Western population control programs? As is evident, population reduction programs have a long history of camouflage and deception. The currently popular idea of seeing population growth in poor countries as humanity's major problem, while hiding the role of the economic order and its leaders in creating this poverty, is, unsurprisingly, propagated, above all, by the rich and powerful.

The billionaire John D. Rockefeller III (1906–1978), grandson of the once richest man in the world and big brother of the US Vice President Nelson Rockefeller and the banker David Rockefeller, and a patron and confidant of Henry Kissinger, had great influence. John D. Rockefeller III founded the Population Council in 1952, a lobby organization for population control that today develops, manufactures, and distributes long-term contraceptives, including copper intrauterine devices, hormonal intrauterine devices, and hormone implants. According to its own statement, 170 million women currently use contraceptives developed by the Population Council.[231]

In 1967, after protracted lobbying, Rockefeller succeeded in organizing an appeal to thirty heads of state, including the US president, whereby "the population problem must be recognized by government as a principal element in long-range planning." The aim of family planning would be "the enrichment of human life" by empowering "man" to "attain his individual dignity and reach his full potential."[232]

The World Bank was also on board. In 1968, Robert McNamara was appointed as its head. He had been a senior official in the statistics office of the US Air Force during World War II where he had increased the efficiency of the bombing of Japanese cities.[233] Later, in the 1960s, as US Secretary of Defense, he organized the bombing of Vietnam. At the World Bank, he launched credit programs for poor countries linked to population reduction measures, i.e., family planning.[234] At the end of the 1970s, McNamara named John Robert Evans (a subsequent chairman of the Rockefeller Foundation), as the head of a new World Bank division of Population, Health and Nutrition, which continued to advance these goals. More recently, from 2013 to 2019, this department was headed by his son, Timothy Grant Evans, a co-player at Event 201.

The US-led World Bank[235] has long been seen as the main sponsor of population control plans. The motives can be found in a 1974 decision of the National Security Council, written under the direction of the then US Secretary of State and concurrent National Security Adviser Henry Kissinger. The paper was long held secret and only became publicly available fifteen years after it was formulated. Under the title "Implications of Worldwide Population Growth for US Security and Overseas Interests," it discusses why many young people in poor countries are a problem:

"The young people, who are in much higher proportions in many LDCs [less developed countries], are likely to be more volatile, unstable, prone to extremes, alienation and violence than an older population. These young people can more readily be persuaded to attack the legal institutions of the government or real property of the 'establishment,' 'imperialists,' multinational corporations, or other—often foreign—influences blamed for their troubles. ... The tensions within the Have-not nations are likely to intensify, and the conflicts between them and the Haves may escalate." [236]

The idea was simple: Fewer rebellious young people offer less resistance and, in general, fewer people in poor, commodity-supplying countries lead to less competition for these commodities. In other words: Countries with fewer people, especially fewer young people who have surplus power and energy, can be exploited and controlled more easily. Because this concept was quite transparent, considerable efforts were made to disguise it. In a further resolution in 1976, the US National Security Council stated the following:

"In the case of less developed countries uncommitted to population programs, our efforts must be fine-tuned to their particular sensitivities and attitudes. In the main, we should avoid the language of 'birth control' in favor of 'family planning' or 'responsible parenthood,' with the emphasis being placed on child spacing in the interests of the health of child and mother and the well-being of the family and community. ... We should lend even stronger support to worldwide efforts for the improved status of women and for their active participation in community and national life. The advancing status of women in parts of Asia and Latin America has evidently been a major factor in promoting successful family planning and in reducing birth rates. ...
"We must nevertheless be selective and low-key in our approaches, lest population programs otherwise be seen

as primarily serving U.S. interests rather than those of other countries. That is why it is so important that the LDC's take more of a lead on population issues at international conferences and at home. We must help ensure that international organizations ... as well as private voluntary organizations, play an active, positive role in support of population programs." [237]

Progress was, however, made quickly. At the end of 1976, with money from the Ford Foundation and the Rockefeller Foundation, a "Program for the Introduction and Adaptation of Contraceptive Technology" (PIACT) was created with the goal of being adapted to the respective cultures of poor countries, thereby increasing its acceptance. The program was founded in Mexico, with a board of directors comprising doctors from Egypt, India, Colombia, and other countries, but it was led from its headquarters in the US city of Seattle.[238]

The organization later changed its name to PATH (Program for Appropriate Technology in Health) and was led for many years by Event 201 co-player Christopher Elias before he moved to the Bill and Melinda Gates Foundation in 2011, where he continues to be responsible for family planning. The above-mentioned organization, Family Planning 2020, is also largely supported by representatives of the respective target countries, but, as already mentioned, is led by Elias, of the Bill and Melinda Gates Foundation, from Washington.

At first glance, everything appears to be self-evident, transparent, and worthy of support. Behind the scenes, however, things look different. As early as the 1970s, the WHO had started to develop a vaccine to prevent pregnancies over a longer period of time. In the 1990s, charges were made in Mexico, Nicaragua, and the Philippines that such a vaccine had been administered to many women without their knowledge through WHO programs under the guise of tetanus vaccinations. The same allegations resurfaced in Kenya in 2014, where they were also substantiated.[239]

The work of large, often private, international organizations to reduce population in selected countries certainly deserves critical examination. Additionally, the issue has become more complex and explosive through the course of technological development. Measures for population control are no longer "only" concerned with controlling the number of births, but, increasingly, also with the registration and monitoring of the biological characteristics and activities of the population.

For many years now, programs for the establishment of a "digital ID" for the unambiguous identification of all people have been continually promoted. Timothy Grant Evans, the Event 201 co-player and ex-WHO executive, provided a personal outlook on the future at a conference on the hundredth anniversary of the Rockefeller Foundation in 2013, at the beginning of his leadership at the World Bank:

> "In Bangladesh, opportunities are emerging for continuous, life-long, portable electronic health records based on unique biometric identifiers assigned at birth as part of a universal vital events and health information system. If this can be done in Bangladesh, why can't it be done globally? Why couldn't every newborn be assigned a Global Health Identification Number—or GHIN? …
>
> "The knowledge of what determines health has grown exponentially and spans the bio-physical including genomes/proteomes to the cognitive and behavioral, to the social structural and environmental. And just as the Rockefeller Officer, Warren Weaver, catalyzed the emergence of

molecular biology in the 20th century, there is a similar opportunity ahead to combine molecular epidemiology with population demographics and global economics and create a new hybrid discipline entitled 'Epidemonnomics.' Epidemonnomics could shed fundamental insights on the diverse range and interactions of health determinants through multi-level trans-national research where the global sampling frame comprises a cool 10 billion individuals!" [240]

Evans' so-called "Epidemonnomics" (which contains the word demon) describes a development that is already being carried out in practice. A national pilot project has been underway in Bangladesh since 2019. Biometric data, such as the fingerprint of each patient, is digitally recorded and linked to other personal information, such as vaccination status. The country's minister responsible for this program proudly noted in a report for the World Economic Forum that by the beginning of 2020, more than a hundred million digital IDs had been created in Bangladesh.[241]

The initiative promoting this implementation of a globally legible digital identity bears the name ID2020[242] and is funded by the Rockefeller Foundation, Microsoft, the management consultancy firm Accenture, and the immunization alliance Gavi, a partnership of pharmaceutical companies, governments, the World Bank, and the WHO, and was launched by the Bill and Melinda Gates Foundation with the goal of providing all persons with access to vaccination.

In the context of ID2020, according to a sympathetic press report from September 2019, comprehensive vaccinations are intended to be used as leverage to establish the concept of digital identity across the board.[243] If this plan is implemented worldwide—which is the long-term plan—it will result in wide-ranging possibilities for the central control of all people thus recorded. The author Norbert Häring explains:

> "The intention of ID2020 is to make it the norm for identity to become partly or entirely independent of national governments. As a result, 'world citizens' become partly emancipated from all governments, except one: the US government. This government, which takes the view, and also enforces it, that it can enact laws which everyone worldwide must abide by, will make people worldwide maximally dependent because their data will then be located on the servers of US companies, in particular the two leading cloud services of Amazon and Microsoft. The technical standards have been determined by these and other US companies and the centrally managed bodies for these identity data are controlled by these US companies.
>
> "Nothing will prevent the US government from instructing Microsoft or Amazon or any of the other US companies that regulate the program's blockchain architecture to read or block the data of individuals or companies, or to manipulate them in a way that incapacitates those affected.
>
> "Even if they wanted to, the governments of the home countries of those affected will not be able to help them. The people are then effectively under the authority of the US government without having any US civil rights. For there is no need to be under any illusions that it will be the US government that will pull the strings. ...
>
> "China, Russia and a few others will oppose this, so that there will be a division of sovereignty across the world. Europe, however, is participating diligently, together with other industrialized countries in the US sphere of influence.

The developing world, dependent on financial assistance from the World Bank, the IMF and the Gates Foundation will join anyway.

"Once cash is abolished, as the Washington-based Better Than Cash Alliance (US government, Gates Foundation, Mastercard, Visa, Citi) is pursuing, together with the instrumentalization of the UN, the surveillance and control of people and companies is almost complete, whether in the sphere of influence of the USA or of China, which is even further along in this respect. After all, digital payments are one of the main areas of application of the digital identity and the field through which its use can be most effectively enforced."[244]

Population control is therefore something different today, more layered and totalitarian than it was fifty years ago. The measures increasingly affect the entire world. Crucially, all these global trends are being massively accelerated by the coronavirus crisis. The virus and the worldwide fear of it provide a welcome opportunity for the realization of such large-scale plans.

8

Impending Collapse: The September 2019 Financial Markets Quake

Before examining the onset of the coronavirus crisis from January 2020 in the following chapters, we should first take a look at a dramatic and little-known event that shortly preceded this outbreak. In September 2019, the US financial markets suffered a threatening crisis, but this information remained largely below the broad public's attention threshold. The German weekly *Die Zeit* wrote on October 1, 2019:

"The crisis came overnight. Banks threatened to run out of money. Central bankers pumped hundreds of billions of dollars into the money market just to prevent the worst happening. All of this sounds like the height of the world financial crisis 11 years ago—but, in fact, it describes the Monday of the penultimate week. An important part of the world's financial system was on the verge of collapse, and the public noticed next to nothing. On the night of September 17, a specific interest rate ... in the US was raised without warning: the rate for banks wishing to borrow in the short term. Normally, the banks in the US are able to borrow money at an interest rate of around two percent ... But this was increased quite suddenly to ten percent. ... The last time central bankers had had to intervene in the repo market was after the demise of the investment bank

Lehman Brothers in 2008. The investment bank's imbalance triggered a state of emergency in this part of the financial system at a time that would have almost led to the collapse of the global economy."[245]

A look at the US Federal Reserve's official balance sheet highlights how this shook the financial markets and led to a reversal in trends.[246] To understand this: At the height of the financial crisis in the fall of 2008, the Federal Reserve had intervened and "printed" a great deal of money (or, more correctly, it bought government bonds and corporate bonds with money it had generated itself). By this time, the confidence of the banks and large investors had collapsed. The Federal Reserve's massive money "printing" (total assets were doubled in weeks) bridged this crisis of confidence among traders and speculators and averted a systemic collapse. In the years that followed, however, confidence never fully returned, balance sheets continued to be inflated, and the instability of the system grew.

A look at the Federal Reserve's balance sheet shows that, from the end of 2017, the central bank began steadily and in small increments to release pressure from this huge bubble. Government bonds and corporate bonds were sold in manageable, regular tranches in the hope that traders' trust among themselves was high enough. This centrally-controlled process had worked well for two years—until September 2019, when just what the newspaper article above describes, actually happened: A rerun of the 2008 collapse, only much larger this time, and just around the corner.

Immediately, the Federal Reserve went into alarm mode and again began "printing" money.[247] The long-term strategy of slowly releasing pressure in small steps had obviously failed. Once again, an uncontrolled systematic collapse loomed. The official balance sheet figures show how massive money "printing" began in September 2019 and continued steadily over the weeks and months that followed—long before the coronavirus.[248] The German financial journalist Norbert Häring wrote about this on January 16, 2020, when the coronavirus was still a side note in the media:

"The Fed has—unconvincingly—justified its intervention with a temporary miscalculation of its own ... On no account could it be concluded that the banks no longer trusted each other. The alleged miscalculation seems to be quite persistent. Four months later, the emergency loans ... are still being extended in unrestrained amounts and an end is not in sight. The Fed keeps the names of the recipients of the loans secret so that they are not burdened with a reputation of neediness. ... Perhaps the central bank-fueled financial market boom is in its final stages before collapse."[249]

From March 2020, in the shadow of the new "health crisis," money was again "printed" on a historically unprecedented scale. A year later, the Federal Reserve's balance sheet total was twice as high as before the September 2019 stock market quake. Crucially, the turnaround clearly had nothing to do with the emergence of the virus, but with the reported loss of confidence in the stock markets in September 2019.[250]

Seen from this perspective, the question arises as to whether the coronavirus crisis that began in January 2020 is not a global diversionary maneuver to allow the managers of the complex international financial system to gain time to secure their power and control. Seen in this light, it could also be a matter of "revolution prevention," because incalculable unrest, such as the yellow vests protests that put the French government under pressure from the end of 2018, can no longer be carried out under the coronavirus regime. Social distancing effectively and sustainably prevents collective protests on the streets. So, everything stays as it is. Perhaps this appears to some to be the last resort to retain power—because the next, now foreseeable financial crash threatens to bring on a political upheaval, of which headstrong politicians like Donald Trump, who are difficult for the elites to control, are only the first warning harbingers.

9

Covid in Davos:
A Virus is Introduced
(January 2020)

On New Year's Eve 2019, the coronavirus crisis began to unfold in the media—initially still cautiously and inconspicuously. The first report on December 31 read as follows:

> "A mysterious lung disease has broken out in the central Chinese metropolis of Wuhan. So far, 27 patients have been identified, the city's Health Commission has reported. The 'People's Newspaper' denied rumors on the Internet that this was a new outbreak of the SARS lung epidemic. The Health Commission has reported that many of the infections could be linked to a visit to the Huanan fish market in Wuhan. The sick are being quarantined. Seven are in a serious condition."[251]

Although this report by the German press agency DPA, which was apparently based on a report from Reuters,[252] which in turn was based on a press release from the Wuhan Health Commission,[253] was published in multiple German media, it did not attract any further attention due to a lack of discernible relevance.

The fact that twenty-seven ill (not dead) people at the other end of the world even led to an agency report in Germany and other western countries needs to be explained. The fact that news agencies found this information worth publishing was unquestionably related to the rumors on the Internet mentioned in the report (spread by whom?), in which it was speculated that the lung disease SARS, which had emerged in 2003 and since disappeared, had reemerged. The SARS phenomenon, which had been in the headlines for a number of weeks then, was still remembered vividly by many. All the initial reports on the "mysterious" lung disease referred to the seventeen-year-old SARS outbreak. It was this context that created the interest.

Control of information was already in place by the time of the first publication. According to a Chinese report dated January 1, 2020, the police in Wuhan were arresting people who were disseminating "false information" on the disease over the Internet that led to "negative social consequences." The police urged the citizens of the city to not believe or circulate rumors and to ensure "a harmless and clean Internet," recommendations that would also soon become popular in Germany.[254]

There was confusion about the onset of the epidemic. In April 2020, reports surfaced in the US and Israeli media that a division of the US Defense Intelligence Agency, the so-called National Center for Medical Intelligence, had already warned its own government, NATO, and the Israeli military of an unfolding epidemic in the Wuhan region in November (!) 2019 that could develop "catastrophically." The intelligence service denied the report.[255] If it was true, however (and the additional confirmation by the Israelis spoke for this), an obvious question would be: How did the secret service come to these findings as early as November, when it seemed that even the Chinese authorities were not aware of the outbreak?

In the first half of January, the issue remained largely unperceived in the Western media. There were isolated reports, but no news stories that stood out. Even when it was first reported on January 9 that the "enigmatic lung diseases in China apparently originated from a previously unknown coronavirus" that had been detected "in 15 of the nearly 60 officially ill persons" in Wuhan, this did not appear in the main evening news in Germany, *Tagesschau*, but only in an online article of the broadcaster.[256] The editors illustrated the text with a photo of the city of Wuhan in dense smog, subtly suggesting that the lung disease might have something to do with the local air pollution.

The fact that a team led by German virologist Christian Drosten from the Berlin Charité had already developed a PCR test for the detection of the virus on January 16, which the WHO immediately recommended to laboratories all over the world,[257] was not initially registered by the media. Drosten later explained the incredible speed of this test development:

> "It began when the first informal information had arrived here between Christmas and the New Year. ... We relied on just a few indications. We had information from social media that this could be a SARS-like virus and so we put two and two together. ... And when, a short while later, colleagues from China made the first genome sequence of this new virus available [January 10], we naturally compared this with all our possible tests and then selected the best ones and continued to work with them. ... We made this test available to colleagues in China, whose names I cannot reveal. They tested it for us and told us that it worked well."[258]

Thus, the impetus for the test development was given by these already mentioned unspecified "Internet rumors" and the effectiveness of the test had been confirmed by anonymous "colleagues in China." None of this was reported in the media in mid-January. At this time, the mysterious disease at the other end of the world was still not a mainstream topic. But, in the meantime, experts in the background were already setting the course for the coming months.

On Friday, January 17, something very strange happened in this context: The Johns Hopkins Center for Health Security, the World Economic Forum, and the Bill and Melinda Gates Foundation issued a joint press release presenting an evaluation of Event 201 and, in particular, the policy recommendations adopted three months earlier. The communication stated:

> "The next severe pandemic will not only cause great illness and loss of life but could also trigger major cascading economic and societal consequences that could contribute greatly to global impact and suffering. Efforts to prevent such consequences or respond to them as they unfold will require unprecedented levels of collaboration between governments, international organizations, and the private sector."[259]

It called for the further development of an international vaccine reserve, the reduction of regulations relating to vaccine development and a stronger fight against misinformation. Particularly strange was that the coronavirus crisis, which was just starting to unfold, was not mentioned at all, even though the information had obviously been released in this context (otherwise it could have been published three months prior, immediately after the end of the drill). In other words, exercise and reality became strangely intertwined.

The enormous and continuing media interest in the virus began abruptly and unexpectedly, exactly three days later, on Monday, January 20, one day before the opening of the World

Economic Forum (WEF), the annual meeting of the world's most important heads of state and leaders of corporations in Davos. On this day, the new virus was also mentioned for the first time in the main edition of the German public television broadcaster *ARD's* evening program, the *Tagesschau*. The two-minute piece was aired at the end of the show after extensive reporting on the upcoming WEF meeting. With the headline "Massive increase in coronavirus cases," presenter Jens Riewa informed the television audience:

"The novel coronavirus in China is spreading with surprising speed. According to official figures, more than 200 people have already developed the lung condition that is caused by the pathogen. In the meantime, three neighboring countries have also reported infections. The World Health Organization has convened a panel of experts to recommend, among other things, possible measures. According to Chinese researchers, the virus can also spread from person to person."

The information that the virus spread "surprisingly fast" was only weakly documented at the time in view of only 200 cases over three weeks. The essential new information was that the disease was transmissible from person to person. Also new was that the Chinese government had radically changed its course from sweeping the subject under the carpet in the beginning to using all its power to declare it a state affair. Beginning on January 20, the Chinese health authorities submitted daily reports containing the latest coronavirus case numbers.[260] The *Tagesschau* also referred to these figures in its report. The short introduction by Jens Riewa was followed by a report from the *ARD's* Peking correspondent, in which he stated:

"Now, right before the New Year's holiday, is peak travel
time in China. Everyone at the Wuhan train station is
being controlled. Medical personnel with thermometers
to measure fever are on duty. ... So far, three people have
died. Most patients have not been seriously ill but suffer
from fever and respiratory problems. ... Today, on the
state television, a researcher reported on people who were
infected although they were not themselves in Wuhan
but have relatives there. 'We can therefore confirm that
there are cases in which the virus was transmitted from
person to person.' This news makes it clear that the spread
of the virus within China is becoming more likely and
controlling the spread of the disease is becoming more
difficult."[261]

Thus, the tone for the coming weeks was set—and not only
on the *Tagesschau*. The media interest at the time, which suddenly surged, is also reflected in the *New York Times'* coverage. Whereas until this point only a few articles on the virus
had been published (January 10, "China reports first death
from new virus"; January 15, "Japan and Thailand confirm
new cases of Chinese coronavirus"; January 17, "Three U.S.
airports to check passengers for a deadly Chinese coronavirus"; January 18, "Deadly mystery virus reported in two new
Chinese cities and South Korea"; and January 20, "China confirms new coronavirus spreads from humans to humans"), the
number of articles virtually exploded with the start of the WEF
meeting in Davos.

On January 21 alone, the opening day of the conference,
five different articles on the coronavirus appeared in the
New York Times, as well as, for the first time, a visual, easy-to-understand "Wuhan Coronavirus Map" to help track the outbreak.

Also on January 21, the WHO published its first coronavirus situation report, which has been published daily since then.[262] The starting signal for the media and the political "coronavirus fire" had been given.

The very next day, something else of consequence for the media transmission of the topic occurred: Johns Hopkins University launched its COVID-19 dashboard, the now-famous online world map showing the geographic distribution of all coronavirus cases as well as the developing trend, with case and death figures being constantly updated. At the launch on Wednesday, January 22, the press release stated:

> "By Wednesday afternoon Eastern time, official Chinese reports said 444 people have been hospitalized and at least 17 had died from novel coronavirus. But the map launched Wednesday by researchers at Johns Hopkins University's Center for Systems Science and Engineering suggests those numbers may be growing faster than national sources have shown. 'We think it is important for the public to have an understanding of the situation as it unfolds, with transparent data sources,' said Lauren Gardner, an associate professor in civil and systems engineering at Johns Hopkins University, who led the team that produced the map. ... Gardner said the map is a 'very simple' collection of reported cases gathered from aggregated local-level sources and requires no modeling. To make the map, Gardner and her team scraped and compiled local Chinese media reports, including CCTV and People's News. Those reports were then translated into English and their locations was [sic] mapped. As new reports come in, the map is updated, Gardner said." [263]

Because it was so accessible and easy to use, the Johns Hopkins dashboard developed a life of its own. Hundreds of media companies around the world used the data and the way it was presented. It was an excellent platform for illustrating the elusive danger of the epidemic. The dashboard also served the media's need for constant news and updates—further fueling public nervousness. From this point on, many editors, media users, and politicians watched the rising curves that were incorporated into almost every article on the subject and gave the impression that one had, at a glance, understood the essentials. "Source: Johns Hopkins" became a familiar word in the media, where numbers from the US were mostly trusted blindly. Through their dashboard, a private US institution had gained international authority over the level of case numbers.

Another big bang also followed on January 22: The Chinese authorities announced that on the following day the ten million inhabitants of the metropolis of Wuhan and several other major cities would be placed under total quarantine. No one would be able to either enter or leave these cities—an action unprecedented in scale. This decision seemed to once again confirm the magnitude of the danger. As an observer, one had to assume that the situation was enormously threatening for the government to take such an extreme step.

Within the WHO political bodies, an attempt was made on the same day to get the organization to declare a "Public Health Emergency of International Concern." This initially failed to gain internal acceptance, but was followed up on January 30.[264]

Worldwide media coverage was now fully focused on the coronavirus. The *New York Times* alone published thirteen articles on the subject on January 23. Among its headlines were: "Fears over new coronavirus grip Davos" and "How China's virus outbreak could threaten the global economy."[265]

At the same time, between January 21 and January 24, almost 3,000 politicians, executives, and journalists, including many of the most powerful heads of state and heads of corporations, were meeting in Davos. This is reminiscent of the Atlantic Storm pandemic scenario of 2005, where the news of an outbreak surprised heads of state at an international conference where the decision-makers were already assembled (see Chapter 4). Here, once more, the corresponding excerpt from the screenplay at that time:

> "On January 13, the eve of the summit, smallpox cases were reported in Germany, the Netherlands, Sweden, and Turkey. The leaders decide to meet for a few hours on the 14th before heading home to deal with the emerging crisis. During the six hour meeting, the transatlantic leaders wrestled with the enormity and rapid pace of the emerging epidemics of smallpox, the tension between domestic politics and international relations, the challenge of controlling the movement of people across borders, and an international shortage of critical medical resources such as smallpox vaccine."[266]

Replacing the word smallpox with coronavirus and January 13 with January 23, one would have landed up pretty much in the reality of 2020.

The annual WEF meeting in Davos is the largest and most high-profile event of its kind. At the end of January 2020, the leaders of the world's most powerful corporations were gathered in Davos. They included the heads of Google, Apple, Facebook, and Microsoft.[267] In addition, the CEOs of the leading pharmaceutical companies Roche, Bayer, Sanofi, and AstraZeneca (the company that, a few months later, sold Germany a vaccine that had not yet been developed for a three-digit million euro amount),[268] and the head of the pharmaceutical group Moderna, whose focus was on the novel RNA vaccine that began being developed at a rapid rate during the coronavirus crisis. Also present were the chairmen of Gavi, The Vaccine Alliance and the CEO of the vaccine research association CEPI, Richard Hatchett, who shortly afterwards coordinated the worldwide vaccine development for COVID-19.[269]

Other guests in Davos included the chief executives of several major banks, as well as BlackRock, Visa, Mastercard, the Rockefeller Foundation, the Atlantic Council, the chairmen of the central banks of a dozen states, numerous editors-in-chief of major media outlets, as well as the heads of states and governments of several countries, including Donald Trump and Angela Merkel.[270]

During an exciting week in Davos, they all had ample opportunity to coordinate their reactions to the crisis—not necessarily specifically on the open stage, but also discreetly, on the fringes of the event. Direction to politicians was given on January 23 in a *New York Times* commentary: "Be ready for anything, and leave it to the experts."[271]

Coinciding with the conclusion of the WEF meeting on January 24, the WHO reported twenty-five coronavirus deaths worldwide.[272] This figure did not fit at all with a threatening "global crisis." And yet, the political decisions described above, their accompaniment in the media, and the general projection of a "new SARS" had created the impression of immense danger.

What is striking in hindsight is that by January 24, when the heads of states and corporations that had gathered in Davos were traveling back home, several crucial elements for the future management of the coronavirus crisis were either already introduced or operational. These included:

→ the PCR test for collecting cases,
→ the WHO daily status reports to inform the public,
→ the COVID-19 dashboard for a graphic representation of
the situation in the media,
→ the political recommendations from the WEF and the
Gates Foundation.

Everything had been prepared for. And indeed, from that point on, the crisis unfolded almost automatically. The huge pandemic machine that had been designed, rehearsed, and prepared for an emergency many years before, was now up and running.

Here again, however, it should be noted that this observation does not yet imply any planning or deliberate development of the pandemic. The process can also be explained as harmless: The institutions involved had simply been drilled for such an outbreak. Virologists were constantly looking for new pathogens, eager to discover them. For twenty years, scientists, like those at the Johns Hopkins University, had done nothing other than warn of bioterrorist attacks and pandemics. If their real potential became apparent, maximum activity would result. The WHO and many other government agencies also merely implemented procedures that had been repeatedly rehearsed, wanting to work as efficiently as possible, make no mistakes, and follow exactly the rehearsed protocols. From this perspective it was, in fact, a kind of machine that, once launched, followed its programmed dynamics.

Thus, so far, the innocuous narration. Nevertheless, other explanations are conceivable. If the pandemic had been deliberately triggered, i.e., if the virus was a bioweapon (as described by the US officer and later coronavirus crisis manager Robert Kadlec, see Chapter 2), then the situation would appear far more complex. It was also conceivable that, in the shadow of a naturally-occurring virus, a similarly acting but far more lethal bioweapon was deployed in deliberately selected locations around the world. By the end of January, these questions could not be answered by the normal observer.

At the time, China appeared to take the threat very seriously. The government began testing its citizens for the virus on a large scale. The daily reported number of cases rose rapidly, just as those who had warned us predicted—from 131 on January 23 to 259 on January 24, then 444, 688, 769 up to 1,771 on January 28. Followed closely by the world's media, the number of new cases reported daily remained in the lower four-digit range for exactly four weeks, until February 20, when the values dropped abruptly—from one day to the next—from 1,749 to 394, and then remained constant in the mid to lower three-digit range for two weeks, before dropping to a barely measurable level at the beginning of March.[273]

What had happened? Had China defeated the pandemic with its rigorous quarantine measures as the media suspected? Or had the Chinese government, after four weeks of diligent testing, quite simply decided to radically reduce the number of tests and "end" the pandemic in this way? Thus, in the absence of a documented virus, people with pneumonia would, in the same way as before the crisis, simply be declared "normal" respiratory disease patients.

This suspicion was difficult to dispel because, unlike other countries, China did not publish verifiable data on the number of daily or weekly tests. At the very least, it seemed hardly conclusive that a rapidly spreading epidemic in a country with over one billion inhabitants and a consistently high number of tests performed would have, after just a few weeks, only nineteen new cases on March 10 or eight new cases on March 23 nationwide! But this is what was officially reported.[274]

Media reports critical of this were the exception and appeared, at best, in niche publications.[275] Almost the full spectrum of media accepted the story of China's success, which was supported by the supposedly neutral Johns Hopkins dashboard. If even the US published the Chinese figures, then the numbers were likely to be correct—at least this seemed to be the unconscious assumption of many.

In addition, the WHO, in a report published on 28 February 2020 by its own investigative commission that had just returned from China, also backed these figures, stating that the conspicuously abrupt decline in new infections was "real" and convincing.[276]

Whatever the truth may have been, China was, at least in the perception of the public, rid of the coronavirus problem, and had shown the world how to react: decisively and severely. This lesson was then followed almost everywhere.

10

Deaths in Europe: Panic and Deception (February 2020)

The first victim of the ongoing media storm that began at the end of January was composure. Following a pernicious media logic,[277] public agitation was ramped up week after week. With every new news article, every case number report, every new expert warning, the public's ability to weigh the situation calmly and reflectively rapidly faded. It became clear that the virus had caught Western society in a situation in which they were exceptionally vulnerable to anxiety and panic.

The previous chain of global insecurities had dragged on for more than 20 years: 9/11, the Iraq War, the financial crisis, the National Security Agency surveillance scandal, Donald Trump. Each of these keywords represented a shock to the world—and the public had not recovered from any of them. On the contrary, they had piled up into a mountain of unresolved trauma. There had long been a question of distrust in the strength and correctness of the Western system. At the beginning of 2020, the Western psyche was experiencing a state of high disruption and susceptibility. Metaphorically speaking, a gust of wind was enough to induce collapse. Or a mere virus.

After China, the unloved social climber, had demonstrated to the world the strength and determination with which it could react, other governments found themselves in a tight spot. In Europe, the disaster found its course when the first two deaths were reported in Italy on Saturday, February 22. Influenced by the continual alarmist reporting of the previous four weeks and the rigorous measures taken by China, the Italian government took frantic action. On the following day it not only instructed schools, universities and businesses to close, but, like the Chinese, also quarantined entire cities. This sent panic in Europe to a new level. Naked fear broke out.

Prime Minister Conte dramatically explained the measures: He did not want to allow Italy to become a "military hospital." This quote was aired on the *Tagesschau* on February 23 and made a deep impression. The fact that a European leader had openly admitted that he was afraid of the mass deaths of his own citizens left no one unmoved. The next day, Italy announced a total of five (!) dead, the *Tagesschau* reported:

> "Following the emergence of the novel coronavirus in Italy, the German government envisages a changed situation in Germany. Health Minister Spahn expects the virus will also spread in this country."[278]

The same television report showed scenes of panic in Italy with shoppers emptying supermarket shelves. A pensioner from Genoa was quoted as saying: "The spaghetti shelves are empty, what is going on here? Not even at the beginning of World War II did such a panic break out!" The nervous reaction of the Italians, conveyed through pictures on television, affected Germany almost instantly. At the same time, the WHO continued to increase its pressure on governments, as reported by the *Tagesschau* on February 25:

> "The World Health Organization is pressuring governments worldwide to prepare for a coronavirus outbreak.

The message from Geneva is that hospital beds, isolation and intensive care units and ventilators must be made ready for use."

This message also did not fail to have an effect. The WHO was considered trustworthy and the mention of isolation wards and ventilators immediately planted nightmarish images of patients dying miserably in people's minds. These images and visions of gloom persisted for weeks, making clear and calm thinking increasingly difficult for many people. The fact that the same report also mentioned in passing that all those deaths registered in Italy in connection with the virus were of people suffering from preexisting conditions, was already lost on the public—it did not fit the rest of the story.

Germany's Federal Minister of Health, Jens Spahn, under pressure from the urgent recommendations of the WHO, as well as from a startled media, was meanwhile addressing the public on an almost daily basis. On February 26, he declared with dramatic seriousness: "We are at the beginning of a coronavirus epidemic in Germany." The point of origin was seven (!) new coronavirus cases in Germany whose path of infection could not be traced. According to Spahn, he was coming increasingly closer to the conclusion that there was no hope the epidemic would pass Germany by. The situation had "changed in the last few hours." He was referring to the seven new cases.[279]

After this appearance, which further heightened general fear in Germany, all hell broke loose. Spahn sent out the message that the deadly virus was approaching rapidly and was basically unstoppable. In the course of the day, the federal government established a crisis management staff as provided for in the national pandemic plan.[280] The media followed suit and launched its very own "pandemic plan": A live blog was launched on *tagesschau.de*, which, from then on, did not rest for weeks and months on end. The first headlines were on February 26:[281]

"New cases in several European countries"
"WHO urges preparation"
"First case in Baden-Württemberg"
"Infection in NRW confirmed"
"Patient in NRW in critical condition"
"Coronavirus again responsible for acute losses on US markets"
"More than 100 new coronavirus cases in South Korea"
"First suspected case in South America"
"Japan: Schools closed in Hokkaido"
"European Chamber of Commerce head warns of 'extreme' consequences"
"Fear of the pandemic pushes DAX down"

On the next day, February 27, in the midst of an increasingly hysterical atmosphere, the Robert Koch Institute (RKI), the German equivalent of the US CDC, held a detailed press conference on the subject for the first time, and thereafter on an almost daily basis. When asked by a reporter why the concern among the authorities was so great, RKI head Lothar Wieler pointed to the particularly high death rate of the virus. "According to the figures we have so far, one has to assume that about one to two percent of people who are infected die from this disease," Wieler said.[282] That would be ten times more than with the normal flu. On its website, the RKI was more cautious than Wieler at the time: "There is currently not enough data available for a final assessment of the severity of the new respiratory disease." A death rate was not reported.[283]

As it turned out later in numerous studies, the fatality rate was in fact many times lower.[284] Doubts surrounding the death rate had already been justified in February, since the high death rate in China could be clearly attributed to the fact that mainly the seriously ill were tested, with those less affected hardly or not documented at all, even though they accounted for more than eighty percent of the cases.[285] The fact that Wieler was aware of this at the time was indicated by an awkwardly worded phrase he used in the press conference:

> "In China, for example, rates are higher than they are outside China. This is probably due to the fact that in China, as a whole …"

At this point, Wieler broke off and paused. He appeared to realize that the logical completion of the sentence ("… more seriously ill people are being tested") would lead to the problematic conclusion that the death rate would actually be lower, meaning the general panic was medically ill-founded. Wieler began again, this time more or less elegantly circumventing the delicate issue:

> "So, it must be said, first of all, that we will of course never find every single infected person. Many people are infected and have no or very few symptoms. In other words, the common denominator, the so-called common denominator, is probably always greater than what we really see. In other words, China will definitely be seeing more serious cases so you will have higher death rates there. This is the explanation for the difference in numbers."[286]

The journalists sitting across from Wieler, from the German newspapers *Bild* and *Süddeutsche Zeitung* to the *New York Times*, either found it difficult to follow the RKI boss at this point or did not realize the significance of his point. In any case, none of those present made a statement or asked for further clarification. Why one would "see more serious cases" in China than in other countries remained unclear. Wieler's statement, however, made sense only if it was understood in such a way that meant China *tested* mainly serious cases, while milder cases, with weak or no symptoms, were not documented. This would, then, artificially push up the death rate. Wieler added:

> "Abroad, we are at a rate of about one percent. It might even be less. These are the current figures. But what is clear is that the rates of the deceased are higher than for the flu. How much higher, we will see when this epidemic is over."[287]

This conclusion, however, was even then not, as Wieler had indicated, at all "clear," but rather an unsubstantiated assertion in the absence of meaningful data. The government was acting on this technical basis. Their arguments were based on a death rate whose extreme exaggeration was already logically clear to the experts at this time. But it also became clear that Wieler was obviously not the one on whose expertise the government based its decisions. Spahn and Merkel had made a political decision to give in to international and media pressure. The RKI, so it seemed, was merely given the task of conveying the "appropriate" facts to the public.

The RKI was not responsible for the report on the excessive death rate. This deception came from higher up, directly from the WHO, which, at the end of February, in answer to the question "What are the symptoms of COVID-19?", informed the world's public on its website:

"The most common symptoms are fever, tiredness, and dry cough. ... About 2% of people with the disease have died." [288]

These sentences were included in a catalogue of answers to frequently asked questions about the virus published by the WHO on February 23. No source was given for the death rate of two percent.

On the same day, the organization reported 77,042 confirmed cases and 2,445 deaths in China in its situation report—a mathematical death rate of 3.2 percent. A total of 1,769 cases were reported for all other countries (one third of which were attributed to mass testing on the Diamond Princess cruise ship and another third to South Korea) and seventeen deaths, resulting in a death rate outside China of one percent.[289] If the figures for China and the rest of the world were added together, the global death rate was 3.1 percent—again a mathematical calculation. How the WHO got to the two percent it mentioned from this remains unclear. The actual number had to be many times lower, since eighty percent of cases remained hidden due to only weak or non-existent symptoms.

The fact that the WHO did not explain these basic epidemiological relationships to the public openly and in an easy-to-understand way from the outset is a clear indication that unrelated political motives were at play. The fear was obviously politically desired and the course towards a state of emergency had already been set.

At the second press conference of the RKI on the following day, February 28, the death rate was classified differently. Wieler was not present, and this time the institute's deputy head, Lars Schaade, explained that there was a strong underreporting of cases in China, which, "according to some writers, could be by a factor of 20, meaning that only five percent of cases have been reported."[290] The internationally reported death rate of two to three percent "would then fall." Moreover, it would not yet be clear how many of the international cases would have taken a serious course. In closing, and in striking contradiction to Wieler the previous day, Schaade said:[291]

> "My assessment would be that this is moving at about the severity of a strong to very strong wave of the flu."

Schaade also said that the RKI did not recommend the wearing of masks in everyday life. When asked, he clarified:

> "This has been investigated a number of times: there is simply no scientific evidence that this makes any sense."[292]

This information did not appear on the *Tagesschau*. The fact that the death rate could be lower by a factor of twenty (!) and thus, according to the RKI, was comparable to that of the flu, was simply not mentioned on the evening news of February 28. Instead, the population was intensively prepared for the implementation of quarantine measures. In one news item, it was explained what the Infection Protection Act would allow the authorities to do and what was required of the public:

> "If a patient shows symptoms of the disease, the local health department will decide whether to quarantine them. ... Quarantine may even be enforced against the will of the persons concerned, but only by a court order. Salaries are generally paid during quarantine. ... Employees who have the opportunity to work at home in their home office during quarantine are obliged to do so."[293]

Thus, it was no longer merely about washing hands and hygiene measures for sneezing and coughing. Much more far-reaching interventions into the private lives of the population were announced. The *Tagesschau* report was accompanied by film footage of people wearing masks in their daily lives—thereby contradicting the RKI recommendation. The message was clear: The virus is extremely dangerous and instructions given by the authorities must be followed.

On that same Friday, February 28, at the end of the week in which Europe had begun to panic, Bill Gates spoke out. On his blog, he published a text with the bold headline: "How to respond to COVID-19."[294] The billionaire's article also appeared in the *New England Journal of Medicine*, one of the most respected and widely read medical journals in the world, under a somewhat more modest title.[295] Gates cautioned that the worrying COVID-19 death rate (!) meant that vaccine development had to now be massively accelerated with the support of public funding. The "partnership" of pharmaceutical companies, governments, and the WHO for vaccine development, CEPI, that he had launched in Davos in 2017, would already be at work. However, it would take billions of dollars from governments to complete the necessary clinical trials and get the vaccines ready for approval:

> "Scientists sequenced the genome of the virus and developed several promising vaccine candidates in a matter of days, and the Coalition for Epidemic Preparedness Innovations is already preparing up to eight promising vaccine candidates for clinical trials. If some of these vaccines prove safe and effective in animal models, they could be ready for larger-scale trials as early as June."[296]

In other words, saving the world was also a billion-dollar deal, and the pressure to successfully conclude the planned vaccine contracts with governments around the world was enormous. In this context, a death rate on the order of the normal flu—as was obvious, suspected by the RKI at the time, and determined by many studies later[297]—was the last thing needed by the companies in question. Without the global fear of millions of deaths, the new vaccines would not sell very well.

Nevertheless, it would be too one-dimensional to look for the motives of political strategy solely in the interests of the pharmaceutical industry. This crisis, and thus the influence of other industries without the same immediate interest, was too big for that. Such a narrowing of perspectives would also not do justice to the person of Bill Gates. On the one hand, Gates was a calculating manager, always striving to lead the fields in which he was active, pushing aside competitors or opponents, whether as the head of a global corporation or a vaccination campaign. Yet, at the same time, this superrich man seemed to be honestly driven by a desire to help world, but remained trapped in a technical tunnel vision that sees only technological and commercial solutions. Almost idealistically, he seemed to be convinced that profit-seeking by faceless and cultureless world corporations could be combined with philanthropy and altruism in a beautiful harmony. This could be viewed as tragic self-deception. But Gates was certainly not an ice-cold villain who simply wanted to make money from the crisis. Rather, he was a powerful player in a multi-layered network of very different interests, all of which were trying to exploit the looming situation of a global state of emergency for their own benefit.

Meanwhile, in Germany, the pandemic "machine" had also reached "operating temperature." On March 2, Jens Spahn, together with a large supporting cast, held a national press conference. Virologist Christian Drosten—who would become a public celebrity in the course of the crisis and who could be regarded in some ways as an equivalent to Anthony Fauci in the US—sat next to him for the first time, together with Lothar Wieler and other professors. The minister openly and with visible pride stated that "today's appearance is part of an intensified communication offensive." An advertising campaign would already be underway in all major newspapers, through special government-produced radio commercials, and on all channels of social media.[298]

Such formulations would be more expected from the marketing manager of a company at an internal board meeting. But to Spahn, who is married to the chief lobbyist of the Burda media group (which publishes *Bunte*, a people/celebrity magazine, and *Focus*, a weekly news magazine), fashionable public relations terminology had apparently long ago become second nature. Politics was not only problem-solving, but also perception management—a crisis should also always be "felt" as a crisis.

After the introduction of the smart "communication offensive," the press conference moved on to the real thing: the danger posed by the virus. Wieler avoided talking again of a death rate of between one and two percent as he had done a few days before. Instead, he cautiously formulated:

> "What is very important is that we do not have sufficient data for a final assessment of the severity of the new respiratory disease. We cannot evaluate the severity sufficiently."[299]

Nevertheless, Wieler's RKI had increased the risk level for the health of the population in Germany to "moderate." Then it was Drosten's turn. After being introduced several times over the previous days as an independent expert on the *Tagesschau*, this was his first significant appearance alongside the government. The virologist also remained cautious:

> "It's almost impossible to say at the moment how dangerous
> the virus is. Danger is not a number. And that's actually the
> reason why we have to provide explanations here, some
> of which we do not have ourselves or are just beginning
> to understand. ... At the moment, we are in the region of
> 0.3 to 0.7 percent mortality."[300]

Drosten did not give a source for these completely new figures, nor was he asked to explain by the journalists who were present:

> "We have many mild cases. This disease is a mild disease.
> It is primarily a cold. ... So, the question is, what are we
> actually getting worried about here?"[301]

The members of the press who were present listened attentively when the virologist explained that even this "cold" could become dangerous if too many people suddenly fell ill and simultaneously burdened the health system. It would therefore be necessary to slow down the spread.

Not mentioned was the fact that a massive overload of doctor's offices and hospitals and many deaths from flu epidemics had been observed time and again, as, for example, at the beginning of 2018, but these had never led to large press conferences, crisis teams, and permanent alarm. The threat of the virus was described as a completely new, unprecedented threat, which, however, could not be substantiated by the numbers. Drosten even acknowledged that the infection rate of the virus, the so-called secondary attack rate, was five to ten percent lower than in an influenza pandemic.[302]

A remarkable admission followed an explosive question from a journalist. A reporter had combined the lower limit of the death rate (0.3 percent) mentioned by Drosten with a statement he had made elsewhere that the virus would affect sixty percent of the population. This would result in at least 150,000 deaths in Germany. Was this kind of mass death really to be expected? Drosten mollified him. The calculations could not be made in this way because:

> "People in Germany die anyway. About 850,000 people die in Germany every year. These people have a very similar age profile to the patients who die from a viral disease like this. It is primarily patients with underlying diseases and older patients who die, which is also how it is with this virus. From a certain point, such a disease moves in the direction of normal processes."[303]

This explanation was astonishing. Wolfgang Wodarg, physician, former politician, and leading critic of the government policy during the coronavirus crisis, argued in the same way and had repeatedly stressed that one should look at excess mortality in order to be able to assess the danger. This made sense because if positively-tested people died at the age of normal life expectancy—as was mostly the case with COVID-19—then, of course, it would have meant that without the virus, these people, as a group, would have died at about the same rate. These kinds of deaths were not grounds for declaring a national emergency.

When Wodarg pointed out this connection, he was dismissed as a dangerous "trivializer" of the alleged danger.[304] When Drosten did the same, it was simply quietly ignored by the media. After all, he was on the side of the government. And the government was protecting its citizens.

11

From Testing Madness to Lockdown (March 2020)

Among the major distinctive features of the coronavirus crisis is the idiosyncratic approach to basic medical concepts. The disease, which Christian Drosten had objectively and correctly described as a "mild cold," was treated by the government and the media in a similar way as Ebola, smallpox or the Plague. They spoke of "infected people," "suspected cases," and "COVID-19 sufferers," whereas in more than eighty percent of the cases they meant people who had a cough, a cold, or simply nothing, the so-called "asymptomatic sufferers."

The limits of language are also the limits of our thinking and because nothing harmless existed in the linguistics surrounding the coronavirus, it also became impossible to think of this particular cold as harmless. Every person who tested positive was nothing less than a potential case for the intensive care unit, a possible super-spreader, a radical death messenger to be separated from society.

Soon the category "recovered" was included in the statistics for those who had tested positive and had evaded death's door. The rapid growth of this number was recorded with a great deal of anxious relief. But hardly anyone asked the obvious question: How could someone who had not previously been ill be "recovered"—as in the vast majority of "cases"?

The PCR test, developed by the team around Drosten, proved the presence of viral matter, not a disease.[305] Many questions remained unanswered. Was the material detected fundamentally capable of reproducing, i.e., capable of causing a disease? Was there a sufficient amount of virus in the respiratory organs of the person being tested to make them ill? Or was the viral load too low for this? The PCR test, with its simple classification of positive and negative could not answer these crucial questions.

In addition, the test had a technically conditioned false-positive rate, whose distortive effect became all the more serious the more the spread of the virus in the population decreased, as was observed from April 2020.[306] A report by the *Deutsches Ärzteblatt (German Medical Journal)* on June 12 concluded that a PCR test, under certain circumstances, would even provide a majority of false results.

"The positive forecast value ... is alarmingly low at 0.30. Seventy percent of the people tested as positive are not positive at all, but they are still required to quarantine."[307]

Two days later, even Jens Spahn acknowledged this problem, without, however, any discernible consequences for the test or the media coverage.[308]

Considered seriously, a positive PCR test result could only be interpreted as a first indication of a health-threatening viral infection. It was not for nothing that many manufacturers pointed out that the test was not suitable for diagnosis but only for research purposes.[309] For a useful diagnosis, further evaluation would be needed. As a rule, however, this did not take place. Instead, in most cases, people relied on what was known as a state-of-the-art test that, after all, the WHO had recommended.

Apart from the flaws of the PCR test, there were also other very different questions. Until the end of March 2020, the influenza virus was much more prevalent in Germany than the coronavirus. According to the RKI's virological monitoring, which is based on data from affiliated medical practices and which has been carried out continuously over many years independently of the coronavirus crisis, the proportion of influenza positives in the samples examined in March 2020 was many times higher than the proportion of coronavirus positives (they were explicitly tested for the pathogen SARS-CoV-2).[310]

With a weekly number of samples in the three-digit range, this was a relatively small study, but, according to the RKI, it was a representative study for Germany. The fact that influenza was more prevalent than coronavirus in March 2020 is an undisputed fact, just as is the fact that influenza is a very deadly disease for high-risk groups. According to estimates of the RKI, more than 20,000 people died in Germany of influenza in each of four winters (!) in the past ten years alone.[311] Influenza and COVID-19 have almost the same symptoms. Without a laboratory test, it is not possible to say which virus a coughing, sneezing, and feverish patient has.[312] In both influenza and in COVID-19 it is pneumonia which usually leads to death.

The resulting problem is obvious: The exploding number of daily tests from the beginning of March (several hundred thousand tests were performed per week) did *not* test for influenza, *only* for the coronavirus. Therefore, it is not only possible, but very likely, that the influenza virus could have been detected in many, if not most of the people who tested positive in March—if only they had been tested for it!

The maximum daily number of deaths from COVID-19 cases in Germany was reported between the beginning and the middle of April.[313] Since it takes about three weeks between the initial infection and death, these people had become infected in March, i.e., at a time when influenza was still many times more widespread than COVID-19. The big question now is: How can we be sure that the "coronavirus" deaths at the time were actually COVID-19 and not influenza? The answer is as simple as it is explosive: A fact-based conclusion is not possible. The assumption that coronavirus alone, and not influenza, triggered all these deaths is pure speculation and is not only unsubstantiated but also highly unlikely.

It can be assumed that at least some of the experts at the RKI, the Federal Ministry of Health, and in the federal government agencies were aware of these connections. The fact that, with the exception of a few outsiders, such as Wolfgang Wodarg, *none* made any public reference to them shows how great the political pressure on this issue has been from the beginning. Every expert from the health institutions responsible for managing the crisis could see, by merely glancing at the news, that the government and the media had committed themselves and that there was no room for contradictions. To stand in the way of the pandemic "machine" required, as far as one's own career was concerned, an almost suicidal idealism. It was better to stay safe within the pack and howl with the wolves—or simply shut your mouth.

This political and public health situation formed the background to the so-called lockdown that was implemented at the end of March 2020—a far-reaching halt to public life such as had never been seen before. The journey into lockdown is briefly outlined below.

On March 4, the Italian government closed all schools and universities and on the following weekend closed off large parts of the country. More than ten million people were not allowed to leave their regions. China's radical measures were being repeated.

On Monday, March 9, the DAX fell as sharply as it had last done after the terrorist attacks of September 11, 2001.

Trading was temporarily suspended on Wall Street. In the evening, the *Tagesschau*, however, only mentioned this briefly because a completely different "major event" had eclipsed these stories in the news: The first two coronavirus deaths in Germany had been recorded. These were an eighty-nine-year-old woman and a seventy-eight-year-old man, who had also been diagnosed with a multitude of preexisting conditions.[314] The fact that the producers of the country's most important news program decided to headline the deaths of two seriously ill elderly people in the day's news was revealing. The media had been literally looking forward to this event: When would the first Germans finally die? Sad, but true. The situation at the time was out of control, not in the medical world, but in the media world.

On March 10, the government in Rome announced that all of Italy was to be a restricted zone. There was a blanket ban on gatherings from Milan to Palermo. No one was allowed to leave their homes except for work, shopping, or to visit the doctor. Historically, this was unprecedented. Restaurants had to close by 6 p.m., social life came to a halt. All of Italy had become a "protected zone," according to the prime minister. With these measures, Italy had outdone even China in terms of severity. Meanwhile, in Wuhan, on the same day, Chinese President Xi Jinping noted joyfully that the epidemic had essentially been contained.

On March 11, 4,000 coronavirus deaths were reported worldwide, while in both China and the severely affected South Korea, the official outbreak numbers were decreasing rapidly. Yet the WHO surprisingly declared the crisis to be a global "pandemic." The reasons for this decision remained opaque and vague. According to the director-general of the WHO, it was thought that too little was being done internationally. For this reason, the

WHO would have "rung the alarm bell": Governments all over the world should become more active and especially prepare their hospitals for the expected onslaught.[315]

In Germany, lockdown was now rapidly approaching. The Bundesliga, the German professional football league and national sanctum, cancelled its games. On the same day, Friday 13, the *Tagesschau* dropped a bomb whose "detonation" was to bring families all over the country to the brink of nervous breakdown in the weeks that followed. *Tagesschau* spokesman Jan Hofer, in a gentle tone of voice and with a slight smile, said the following:

"Good evening ladies and gentlemen, I welcome you to the Tagesschau. Millions of parents in Germany will have to take over the care of their children themselves from the beginning of next week. Almost all federal states have decided to close schools and day care centers or have stopped giving classes. The aim of this is to prevent the rapid spread of the coronavirus."

With this decision the government had completely pulled the plug on normal life in the country. Without childcare, the lives of working parents had been turned upside down. A situation that was manageable or could be tolerated in the upper middle classes—like the families of many journalists and politicians—as a mere "inconvenience," or even "finally, some family time," often meant existential chaos for employees and freelancers with low incomes and young children. The government remained conspicuously blind to this. Apart from some good advice, little help came from Berlin.[316]

In addition, visits to old age homes were prohibited and their residents, who were in any case already socially distanced, became completely isolated and left to their loneliness—a punishment so severe for these people it could hardly be imagined. It was one thing to protect at-risk groups, particularly the elderly, with special precautions, but to impose blanket bans on visits and thus turn old age homes into a kind of "isolation prison" was something quite different. The crisis clearly showed that the people were seen as a willingly manipulable human mass, all the more so if they were old and helpless. Children and old people had been dealt a bad hand.

The next day, Saturday, March 14, the new edition of the weekly news magazine *Der Spiegel* appeared with a cover photograph of an emergency doctor in protective clothing standing between the tarpaulins of a hospital tent. The headline read: "Are We Ready?" It felt as if the country was on the verge of the end of the world, while the reality in Germany on this date was a total of eight (!) coronavirus deaths. *Der Spiegel* author and Relotius[317] supporter,[318] Ullrich Fichtner, did not allow himself be fooled by such triviality. Full of gloomy, prophetic warnings, he raved:

> "When the dead are counted, the system will have to ask itself some unpleasant questions. How could governments and states have ignored the rising danger? And why were they incapable of decisive action until the very end?"[319]

In actual fact, quite different questions were being asked only a few weeks later.

On the same day, with surprising speed and severity, the city of Berlin began to emulate Italy. The Berlin senate ended public life in the capital by simple decree. All pubs, clubs, fairs, cinemas, theatres, and even the churches, who accepted this, were forced to close. In addition, gatherings of more than fifty people were prohibited, including all political demonstrations—a frontal attack on the constitution. In the media, this furious authoritarian approach was awkwardly referred to as "shutdown," a term previously known only in the US when disjointed members of Congress could not agree on the adoption of a common budget and therefore had to close public institutions, blocking the country, which became a hostage of overwhelmed politicians. In this respect, the word was appropriate.

The home stretch to the lockdown (another clumsy term for the grotesque idea of placing entire countries in quarantine) that was announced a week later was illustrated by the following headlines from the *Tagesschau* newsroom, published during the week of Monday, March 16, through Friday, March 20:

"The DAX crashes" (March 16)
"France under curfew" (March 17)
"RKI classifies danger as 'high'" (March 17)
"No curfew—not yet" (March 18)
"Merkel demands discipline in coronavirus crisis" (March 18)
"National curfew approaching" (March 20)

During the same week, the now famous shock-value pictures from northern Italy were also shown. On March 19, the *Tagesschau* opened with footage of an endless column of military trucks driving through the town of Bergamo at dawn. *ARD's* Italy correspondent explained:

"This morning in Bergamo: a frightening picture. An entire convoy of military vehicles removing the dead to the crematoriums at dawn. The facilities of the city cemetery, however, are said to have not been able to cope with the onslaught. Italy, the European nation hardest hit by the coronavirus, has more deaths than China, with officially just over 3,400 coronavirus victims. Italy has thus become the new world center for COVID-19."

This was followed by pictures of immobile patients on ventilators in intensive care:

"In the hospitals of Northern Italy, doctors and nurses are talking about 'war.' The number of people being admitted is so high in many places that it is no longer possible to care for them all. They must decide who they help and who they do not—decisions of life and death. A nurse tells us that there are so many victims that there is hardly any time to save them."

These upsetting images and the dramatic accompanying text were deeply imprinted into the collective mindset of the sixteen million viewers who watched this edition of the *Tagesschau*. Weeks and months later, they were still confronting critics of the coronavirus measures with the argument, always delivered in a tone of impatient outrage: "How can you play down the virus in this way? Haven't you seen the pictures of the dead and dying in Italy?"

This segment—and other similar ones—had an incredible effect. One could almost describe its viewers as having experienced trauma. Their primal fears had been directly addressed and deep emotions were aroused. The pictures did not let go of those who had seen them. It was impossible to counter the shock these pictures caused with objective arguments.

In actual fact, the piece was highly manipulative, as it tacitly supported three speculative or even false assumptions. The first was that only the new virus was responsible for the thousands of deaths; the second was that those people would not have died if they hadn't contracted the virus and would have still lived long lives; and the third was that the health care system in Italy otherwise functions well and is normally not overburdened by influenza outbreaks and that the coronavirus alone was responsible for this collapse.

None of this could be substantiated. Italy already had serious flaws in its health system, partly as a result of the austerity measures following the financial crisis.[320] There were four times fewer intensive care beds per inhabitant than in Germany.[321] The stress limit in the hospitals was thus reached four times faster. Two years earlier, following the mass deaths of the 2018 flu epidemic, the hospitals in Lombardy were already on the verge of collapse, unnoticed by the world press.[322] "Who," one might sarcastically ask, "would be interested in the social hardships of an unruly, bankrupt country?"

As far as the causes of death were concerned, these were far from clear. According to a detailed study of 2,000 deaths by the Italian National Institute of Health from March 17 (of which the *ARD* correspondent could therefore have known at the time of his report), ninety-nine percent of the deceased who had tested positive for the coronavirus had suffered from one or more preexisting conditions and forty-nine percent had suffered from three preexisting conditions. Only three of the deceased had no preexisting conditions. The average age of the deceased was eighty years, which roughly corresponds to the average life expectancy. Only seventeen of the 2,000 deceased were younger than fifty.[323] Walter Ricciardi, the scientific adviser to the Italian Minister of Health, admitted at the end of March:

"The manner in which we record deaths in our country is very generous in the sense that all the people who die in hospitals with the coronavirus are considered to have died from the coronavirus."[324]

These reports were, therefore, highly questionable because preexisting conditions would normally be statistically recorded as the cause of death. For example, if people have been suffering from cancer for years and contract pneumonia in the last days of their lives, they are still considered to have died from cancer.[325] This principle was turned upside down during the coronavirus crisis, not only in Italy, but also in Germany. This, alone, should be considered an incredible scandal—but it was accepted with a shrug by the government and the media.[326]

In the context of respiratory diseases, it is noteworthy that the air quality in the crisis area of Northern Italy is worse than in almost any other region in Europe. This is evidenced on satellite images of the region.[327] Italian researchers noted a direct link between the high levels of air pollution and the coronavirus cases.[328]

None of this was mentioned in the *Tagesschau* report. The conclusions would have hardly fit their story, even though it described a completely different, less exciting, but no less tragic account: Seriously ill people, who had been living for a long time in a polluted environment, were admitted to substandard hospitals at the end of their lives, where, suffering additionally from a respiratory illness, they died at an average age of eighty.

If these people had not been tested for the coronavirus, the hospitals would have been just as overcrowded, but the talk would instead have been of a very bad flu season. This would not have particularly interested anyone abroad, just as hardly anyone had been interested in 2018. Nationwide emergency measures would not have been considered. For what reason? The problem was clearly not a single, individual common cold virus, but a polluted environment and an ailing, underfunded health system.

In 2018, hospitals in other countries had collapsed as well, for example in the US, where in January of that year flu patients were cared for in hospital tents in parking lots! In this case, the health system had also suffered funding setbacks and could no longer cope with the onslaught of the sick.[329] In Germany, too, there were dramatic situations in the emergency services at the time, which, according to doctors, were at times no longer manageable.[330] This had not led to crisis measures and emergency resolutions. Without a killer virus, the suffering of people who could not afford private treatment and who depended on the public system was, unfortunately, mostly uninteresting to the government, and often also to the media.

The final steps to the lockdown were, therefore, child's play. People's fear for their own lives and the lives of their loved ones completely dominated their thoughts. The pictures from Italy not only unsettled many, but left them afraid of dying. With such a softened-up public, governments could do anything. And that is what they did.

On March 20, Bavarian Minister-President Markus Söder imposed a curfew. Leaving one's own home in Bavaria was from now on only allowed for "valid reasons," alone, or, at most, accompanied by one's family. Söder explained that he wanted to protect the people, "even from themselves."[331] The guardian state was taking shape. Society was parceled into tiny family groups that were no longer allowed to meet. It could not have been a more inhuman environment.

All this was justified by an ever-increasing number of cases that, at the time, had tripled. While 8,000 new cases were reported in the previous week, the number rose to 24,000 in the week that ended with the lockdown. The danger thus seemed tangible and clear to everyone. What remained hidden was only made public through research carried out by the magazine *Multipolar* on March 28: In this same period of time, the number of tests had also tripled, from 130,000 to 350,000. The actual increase in the number of cases relative to the number of tests was only one (!) percentage point: Between March 9 and March 15, six percent of the subjects tested positive for the virus compared with seven percent between March 16 and March 22. This "rapid" increase represented the "exponential growth" of the epidemic that everyone was talking about. It was a breathtaking deception![332]

On Sunday, March 22, the public still had no inkling of this since the RKI was not yet publishing figures for the number of tests conducted. On that day, Angela Merkel announced that the virus was continuing to spread "with alarming speed in our country," which is why the hospitals were being prepared "for an expected large increase in the number of cases."

She subsequently announced the so-called "guidelines for behavior and freedom of movement," agreed upon by the federal government together with the minister-presidents of the states—but without the participation of parliament—with which all citizens of the country "must comply." The meeting of more than two people in public was prohibited, a minimum distance between people in public of 1.50 meters was made mandatory, and all restaurants were to close. According to Merkel, these were "not recommendations, but rules," whose observance would be monitored: "Law enforcement agencies will be checking, and where they find evidence of violations, there will be consequences and penalties." According to Merkel, however, some freedoms were to remain: "The road to work remains open, of course."[333]

The dark dystopia of a frightened, unfree society seemed to have been realized. All it had taken was a few weeks of over-heated, uniform media coverage freed from doubt, and a policy that made it its compass.

Epilogue:
About Death—and Error

When one looks at the events from a distance, what remains? Every year, millions of people die, under very different circumstances and at very different ages. Many of these deaths are largely and unquestioningly accepted in the public debate because we have become accustomed to them, whether the deaths are through starvation, war, environmental toxins, transportation, alcohol, influenza, or hospital infections. Obviously, it is not right to accept preventable deaths. Nothing should be more important than preventing such suffering, which is never only individual but also weighs heavily on families, friends and the entire social circle of the deceased.

Causes of death cannot be ranked by importance. Every life must be protected, and old people in particular deserve respect, support, and attention. Nevertheless, age of death does play a role. Losing one's life at the age of five, or at eighty-five, is not the same thing. This difference is particularly evident in poor countries. According to UNICEF, 15,000 children under the age of five die every day (!) from hunger or preventable diseases—an ongoing catastrophe for which there is no international crisis, no *ARD* news bulletin, no daily live ticker, and no triple-digit, billion-dollar aid program from Western governments.[334]

The coronavirus has absurdly narrowed the view of many people (and the media). It is understandable that triage (the decision concerning which people in an emergency are to be helped first) is rejected as an unethical breach of taboo, and it is understandable that one is deeply shocked when such a selection process in hospitals is reported. Nevertheless, we should not close our eyes to the fact that this triage takes place on many levels, daily and worldwide—just not in the eyes of the media. Globally speaking, every person who dies of hunger in Africa is a victim of triage. They were not helped, even though help might have been possible.

The furor over the deaths of the elderly in the spring of 2020 was strangely disproportionate to the otherwise lack of interest in them. The circumstances in which the elderly are cared for, even in a rich country like Germany, are largely catastrophic. This could be changed, but nothing is being done. It seems that, if possible, the elderly should leave society alone with their suffering. The subject is shied away from. Old is out. In the sudden exuberant political activism, with all the media watching, one could see compensation for one's own bad conscience toward these people: Look here, we are really doing everything for them now!

My own father lived to the age of eighty-nine and I am very happy I had the chance to spend so much time with him until the end. But life is finite, and this end should, above all, be peaceful, dignified, and surrounded by family. How humane is it to have an eighty-five-year-old with severe preexisting conditions artificially ventilated in the event of an additional bout of pneumonia, and to separate them from their family members in order to extend their lives for a few (lonely) weeks? And how often does this happen only because there is no DNR (do-not-resuscitate order) or living will, so that no one is there to take responsibility for this decision?

Death hurts, and modern society, blinded between the poles of fear, a feasibility mania, and belief in technology, can no longer stand this pain. Dying is to be outsmarted or "treated away," or at least made to disappear somehow.

This is one aspect of the crisis, perhaps the most fundamental. Another is the rift that has opened up within society, not only in Germany, but around the world—between "mask-wearers" and "coronavirus critics" (a strange term created by the media that actually implies "government critics"), between those concerned about the next wave of the infection and those concerned about their freedom and their fundamental rights. There appears to be no consensus. In April 2020, Ulf Roeller, a correspondent for the German television broadcaster *ZDF*, gave an enlightening report from China on Markus Lanz's talk show. When asked by Lanz what a "return to normality" in China meant, he had the following to say:

"What scared me most, and this is perhaps also an issue which is of great interest to the German viewers, is the lightning speed with which the 'surveillance state' emerged. For every move you wish to make you have to download an app. ... The public's health fears are being used to allow this massive surveillance to take place. ... Most of the Chinese we've spoken to think it's great. Their fear of a new wave of infection is so great that even being controlled by the state is not seen as a restriction of their freedom but something positive that is there to protect them."[335]

In Germany, the government introduced the contact-tracing Corona-Warn-App in June 2020, which, three weeks later, had already been downloaded fifteen million times.[336] In their search for security, people voluntarily participate in systems in which the potential for abuse can reach dizzying heights as the number of participants increases. The debate around the introduction of a digital proof of immunity that regulates access to areas of public life and divides society into two classes of "vaccinated" and "dangerous" had, as of July 2020, only just begun in Germany.

Fear is dividing the country: Some trust the government, others warn against it. The biggest problem with discussions across the divide seems to be the threat of loss of face. Acknowledging the arguments of skeptics would mean admitting to having been wrong, perhaps even to having been manipulated. In a society that does not tolerate mistakes and in which everybody wants to do everything correctly and preferably perfectly, this is not an appealing option. Being wrong has become unacceptable. Many journalists and executives see making a mistake as unprofessional—they know the ropes and what is going on and they won't allow themselves to be fooled.

However, quite independently of the coronavirus crisis, it is exactly those "unblemished" figures in politics, business, and the media, who have become blind to their own opportunism, and who are leading the world, one step at a time, into chaos. Society however, and that is all of us, needs the doubts, the pause to reflect, the ability to change our minds, probably more urgently than ever before.

INDEX
AND
NOTES

NOTES

PREFACE TO THE ENGLISH EDITION

1 From September 2020 to February 2021 the book was on the bestseller list of *Der Spiegel* for nonfiction books in Germany.

2 Paul Schreyer, "Pandemic Simulation Games—Preparation for a New Era?" Wissen ist Relevant (Knowledge is Relevant), November 20, 2020. For the English version, the video of the lecture has been subtitled and dubbed, https://wissen-ist-relevant.de/vortrage/paul-schreyer-pandemic-simulation-games-preparation-for-a-new-era/

INTRODUCTION

3 Lawrence K. Altman: "Is This a Pandemic? Define 'Pandemic,'" *New York Times*, June 8, 2009. Excerpt: "A number of doctors ask why health agencies do not declare seasonal influenza a pandemic when it spreads around the world. But Dr. Osterholm, [Dr Michael T. Osterholm, director of the Center for Infectious Disease Research and Policy at the University of Minnesota], said that 'you can't use the terminology for just worldwide transmission, because if you did that, you would say every seasonal flu year is a pandemic.'"

4 Elizabeth Cohen: "When a pandemic isn't a pandemic," CNN, May 4, 2009. Excerpt: "Until Monday morning, the WHO had a definition on its Website saying that a pandemic flu causes 'enormous numbers of deaths and illness.' After a CNN reporter pointed this out, WHO spokeswoman Natalie Boudou called back to say the definition was in error and had been pulled from the WHO Website."

5 Peter Doshi: "The elusive definition of pandemic influenza," *Bulletin of the World Health Organization*, Vol. 89, No. 7, pp. 532–538, July 1, 2011. Excerpt: "Since 2003, the top of the WHO Pandemic Preparedness homepage has contained the following statement: 'An influenza pandemic occurs when a new influenza virus appears against which the human population has no immunity, resulting in several simultaneous epidemics worldwide with enormous numbers of deaths and illness.' However, on 4 May 2009, scarcely one month before the H1N1 pandemic was declared, the web page was altered in response to a query from a CNN reporter. The phrase 'enormous numbers of deaths and illness' had been removed and the revised web page simply read as follows: 'An influenza pandemic may occur when a new influenza virus appears against which the human population has no immunity.' Months later, the Council of Europe would cite this alteration as evidence that WHO changed its definition of pandemic influenza to enable it to declare a pandemic without having to demonstrate the intensity of the disease caused by the H1N1 virus. ... The startling and inevitable conclusion is that despite ten years of issuing guidelines for pandemic preparedness, WHO has never formulated a formal definition of pandemic influenza. ... Statements from WHO, such as 'Is this a real pandemic. Here the answer is very clear: yes,' suggest that pandemics are something inherently natural and obvious, out there in the world and not the subject of human deliberation, debate and changing classificatory schemes. But what would and would not be declared a pandemic depends on a host of arbitrary factors such as who is doing the declaring and the criteria applied to make such a declaration."

PROLOGUE: FALSE GUIDING LIGHTS

6 Elon Musk: "The Case For Mars," July 9, 2013, youtube.com/watch?v=Ndpxuf-uJHE

7 Mark Harris: "SpaceX plans to put more than 40,000 satellites in space," *New Scientist*, October 17, 2019.

8 Brian Berger: "SpaceX Confirms Google Investment," *Space News*, January 20, 2015.

9 Shannon Hall: "As SpaceX Launches 60 Starlink Satellites, Scientists See Threat to 'Astronomy Itself,'" *New York Times*, November 11, 2019.

10 Christoph Seidler: "Spacex startet geheimnisvollen Spionagesatelliten" ("SpaceX Launches Mysterious Spy Satellites"), *Der Spiegel*, May 1, 2017.

11 Norbert Häring: "Die totalitäre Horrorvision des Weltwirtschaftsforums wird wahr gemacht" ("The World Economic Forum's totalitarian horror vision is realized"), *norberthaering.de*, April 8, 2020.

12 Nikolai Berdjajew: "Das Reich des Geistes und das Reich des Caesar" ("The Empire of the Spirit and the Empire of Caesar"), Holle Verlag, 1952, p. 56f.

13 Hauke Ritz: "Technologie der unfreien Welt—Teil 1: Der Quellcode" ("Technology of the Unfree World—Part 1: The Source Code"), *Multipolar*, July 6, 2020.

14 *ARD Tagesthemen*: "Bill Gates über Corona-Impfstoff" ("Bill Gates on the Coronavirus Vaccine"), Interview conducted by Ingo Zamperoni, April 12, 2020.

15 Peter C. Gøtzsche: "Tödliche Medizin und organisierte Kriminalität: Wie die Pharmaindustrie das Gesundheitswesen korrumpiert" ("Deadly Medicine and Organized Crime: How the Pharmaceutical Industry Has Corrupted Healthcare"), Riva, 2019.

16 Michael Hanfeld: "Aus der Nähe sehen sie ganz friedlich aus" ("Up close they look quite peaceful"), *Frankfurter Allgemeine Zeitung*, September 19, 2014.

17 In 2013, Christoph Keese, one of the senior managers of the German Axel Springer Group, spent six months in Silicon Valley on behalf of the media company for research purposes. In his subsequent report, he describes how transhumanist future scenarios have "developed into a kind of corporate mission statement in wide circles." Christoph Keese: "Silicon Valley. Was aus dem mächtigsten Tal der Welt auf uns zukommt" ("Silicon Valley. What's in store for us from the most powerful valley in the world"), Knaus, 2014, p. 271.

18 Werner Pluta: "Elon Musk will Mensch und KI vereinen" ("Elon Musk wants to merge humans with AI"), *Golem*, July 17, 2019.

19 Philipp von Becker: "Der neue Glaube an die Unsterblichkeit. Transhumanismus, Biotechnik und digitaler Kapitalismus" ("The New Faith in Immortality. Transhumanism, Biotechnology and Digital Capitalism"), Passagen Verlag, 2015, p. 14.

20 Thomas Bauer: "Die Vereindeutigung der Welt. Über den Verlust an Mehrdeutigkeit und Vielfalt" ("The Unambiguation of the World. On the Loss of Ambiguity and Diversity"), Reclam, 2018, p. 27ff.

21 Michael Butter: "Nichts ist, wie es scheint. Über Verschwörungstheorien" ("Nothing is as it seems. About conspiracy theories"), Suhrkamp, 2018, p. 37f.

22 Michael Meyen: "Kniefall vor der Wissenschaft" ("Kneeling before Science"), *Medienrealität*, March 26, 2020.

23 The virologist Christian Drosten has a similar role in Germany to Anthony Fauci in the US in terms of both his public influence and his arguments. The physician and former politician Wolfgang Wodarg, on the other hand, is a leading critic of government policy during the coronavirus crisis in Germany.

24 Avaaz: "Ärzte schlagen Alarm wegen Infodemie auf Social Media" ("Doctors sound alarm over infodemic on social media"), May 7, 2020; Gustav Theile: "Virologen beschweren sich über Facebook, Twitter und Google" ("Virologists complain about Facebook, Twitter and Google"), *Frankfurter Allgemeine Zeitung*, May 7, 2020.

25 Charles Eisenstein: "The Coronation," *charleseisenstein.org*, March 27, 2020.

26 Hauke Ritz: "Technologie der unfreien Welt—Teil 1: Der Quellcode" ("Technology of the Unfree World—Part 1: The Source Code"), *Multipolar*, July 6, 2020.

DELUSION AND REALITY: DEALING WITH CONSPIRACY THEORIES

27 Ulrich Teusch: "Katastrophengesellschaft in Bestform—vorläufige Überlegungen" ("Disaster Society at its Best—Preliminary Reflections"), *Multipolar*, April 7, 2020.

28 Andreas Wehr: "Der Schlaf der Vernunft gebiert Ungeheuer" ("The sleep of reason gives birth to monsters"), *andreas-wehr.eu*, May 22, 2020.

29 "'Betrug und Verschwörung' im Abgasskandal: US-Justiz klagt früheren VW-Chef Winterkorn an" ("'Fraud and conspiracy' in the emissions scandal: US justice indicts former VW CEO Winterkorn"), *DerTagesspiegel*, May 4, 2018.

30 Ulrich Teusch, "Verschwörung gegen Corbyn" ("Conspiracy against Corbyn"), *Multipolar*, June 29, 2020.

31 Horst Clages: "Kriminalistische Hypothesenbildung" ("Criminal Hypothesis Formation") in "Der Rote Faden: Grundsätze der Kriminalpraxis" ("The Common Thread: Principles of Criminal Practice"), Kriminalistik Verlag, 2016, p. 197ff. Excerpts: "Criminal hypothesis formation is ... a process that affects the entire police operational and investigative process" (p. 198); "The formation of criminal hypotheses is an indispensable basis for the subsequent investigation planning as well as for the progress of the investigative action to clarify and prove the crime and the perpetrator, as far as there are unsolved facts and open questions" (p. 205).

32 Wissenschaftliche Dienste des Deutschen Bundestages (German parliament's research office): "'Verschwörung' im US-amerikanischen Strafrecht und § 30 Abs. 2, 3. Alt. StGB im Vergleich" ("Comparing 'Conspiracy' in US Criminal Law and § 30 para. 2, 3. alt. StGB"), report WD 7-187/07, September 28, 2007.

33 Carsten Forberger: "Wenn Fakten zu Verschwörungstheorien werden" ("When Facts Become Conspiracy Theories"), *Multipolar*, May 27, 2020.

34 For this reason, the term is also conceivably ill-suited for defending scientific thought.

35 Jack Bratich, "Conspiracy Panics. Political Rationality and Popular Culture," State University of New York Press, 2008, p. 3.

36 NATO's GLADIO program, which coordinated special military forces throughout Western Europe during the Cold War, included hundreds of operatives and confidants. Some of them were involved in staged terrorist attacks. Yet the conspiracy managed to remain secret for decades—from the 1950s until 1990, when Italy's Prime Minister Andreotti finally revealed its existence. The *New York Times* quoted President Franscesco Cossiga as saying, "I admire the fact that we have kept the secret for 45 years." Clyde Haberman, "Evolution in Europe; Italy Discloses Its Web Of Cold War Guerrillas," *New York Times*, November 16, 1990.

37 Jack Shafer: "Miller Time (Again)—The *New York Times* owes readers an explanation for Judith Miller's faulty WMD reporting," *Slate*, February 12, 2004. Excerpt, quoting Miller: "My job was not to collect information and analyze it independently as an intelligence agency; my job was to tell readers of the *New York Times* as best as I could figure out, what people inside the governments who had very high security clearances, who were not supposed to talk to me, were saying to one another about what they thought Iraq had and did not have in the area of weapons of mass destruction."

38 Thomas Kruchem: "Internationale Schiedsgerichte—Gefahr für Menschenrechte und Umwelt?" ("International Arbitration Courts—Danger for Human Rights and the Environment?"), *SWR 2*, June 2, 2020; Norbert Häring: "Schiedsverfahren für Investoren: Ein führender Schiedsrichter plaudert aus dem Nähkästchen" ("Arbitration for Investors: A Leading Arbitrator Chats from the Inside"), *norberthaering.de*, July 25, 2018. Excerpt: "It looks like a legal system on the surface, but it only looks that way. There are no hard, reliable rules. Submissions, motions, oral arguments, taking of evidence, and proceedings have little in common with what one sees in a normal court proceeding. ... Speculation and sloppy newspaper articles pass for evidence. Misrepresentations of facts and gross misquotation of authority are legion. When they are discovered, there is usually no punishment."

BIOSECURITY AND THE POLITICS OF FEAR

39 Rebecca Beerheide: "Hans-Ulrich Holtherm: Neu im Bundesgesundheitsministerium" ("Hans-Ulrich Holtherm: New in the Federal Ministry of Health"), *Deutsches Ärzteblatt*, Issue 11/2020, March 13, 2020; Jens Spahn on February 27, 2020 at a Federal Press Conference: "We already decided two, three months ago that there will be a new department in the Federal Ministry of Health, a department for health security, because we have noticed in recent years that this topic—how we prepare for situations like this and how we are networked on both a European and international level—has become increasingly important ..." twitter.com/phoenix_de/status/1233020676476473344

40 NATO Disease Surveillance Seminar, *Wehrmedizin und Wehrpharmazie*, Issue 2011/3, December 5, 2011.

41 Uwe Henning: "Als Generalarzt ins Gesundheitsministerium" ("As Surgeon General to the Ministry of Health"), *bundeswehr.de*, March 26, 2020.

42 Lisa Keränen: "Biosecurity and Communication," in: Bryan C. Taylor, Hamilton Bean (eds.), Handbook of Security and Communication, Routledge, 2019, pp. 223–246. Excerpt: "While medicine, war, and security have always been connected and configured in relation to one another, the recent re-drawing of boundaries between domains of medicine and national security subsumes public health under the security state. ... The institutionalization of biodefense may encourage an exaggerated, open-ended climate of crisis in which ethical deliberations are hurried, obscure, or absent altogether. Such a climate would perpetuate social choices that focus on highly-visible and visceral threats whose actual contribution to the burden of disease is negligible." (The last two sentences quote Keränen from: Nicholas B. King, "Security, disease, commerce: Ideologies of post-colonial global health," *Social Studies of Science*, December 1, 2002.)

43 According to Prof Matthew Meselson in 1967, quoted in: Seymour Hersh: "Reporter. A Memoir," Allen Lane, 2018, p. 68.

44 UN Office for Disarmament Affairs: "The Biological Weapons Convention. An Introduction," 2017, unog.ch/bwc

45 Elinor Langer: "CBW: Weapons and Policies," *Science*, Vol. 155, pp. 299–303, January 20, 1967; Seymour Hersh: "Chemical and biological warfare. America's hidden arsenal," Bobbs-Merrill, 1968.

46 Linda Hunt: "US Coverup of Nazi Scientists," *Bulletin of the Atomic Scientists*, Vol. 41, April 1985, Issue 4, pp. 16–24; Annie Jacobsen: "Operation Paperclip: The Secret Intelligence Program that Brought Nazi Scientists to America," Back Bay Books, 2014.

47 Brandi Altheide: "Biohazard: Unit 731 and the American Cover-Up," University of Michigan-Flint, March 2013, umflint.edu/sites/default/files/groups/Research_and_Sponsored_Programs/MOM/b. altheide.pdf; Eamonn Fingleton: "Imperial Japan's Abominable Dr. Death, And The Most Disgraceful War Crime 'Amnesia' In History," *Forbes*, March 9, 2014.

48 Seymour Hersh: "The secret arsenal," *New York Times Magazine*, August 25, 1968.

49 "Secrecy Over Cold War WMD Tests," *CBS News*, July 1, 2003.

50 Seymour Hersh: "Reporter. A Memoir," Allen Lane, 2018, p. 96.

51 Ibid.; Tom Shanker: "Investigations Of Chemicals Will Continue," *New York Times*, July 12, 2003.

52 Seymour Hersh: "The secret arsenal," *New York Times Magazine*, August 25, 1968.

53 Seymour Hersh: "Reporter. A Memoir," Allen Lane, 2018, p. 98.

54 "Army Report Details Germ War Exercise In N.Y. Subway in '66," *Washington Post*, April 22, 1980.

55 National Research Council: "Toxicologic Assessment of the Army's Zinc Cadmium Sulfide Dispersion Tests," Appendix A: Historical Background of the U.S. Biologic-Warfare Program, National Academies Press, 1997; Victor Ferreira: "U.S. secretly tested carcinogen in Western Canada during the Cold War, researcher finds," *National Post*, October 6, 2017.

56 Eric Salter: "Cold War radiation testing in US widespread, author claims," *AP*, October 2, 2017.

57 Ibid.

58 Lisa Martino-Taylor: "Behind the Fog. How The US Cold War Radiological Weapons Program Exposed Innocent Americans," Routledge, 2017.

59 Lisa Martino-Taylor: "The Manhattan-Rochester Coalition, Research on the Health Effects of Radioactive Materials and Tests on Vulnerable Populations without Consent in St. Louis," University of Missouri-Columbia, 2012.

60 Quoted in Eric Salter, "Cold War radiation testing in US widespread, author claims," *AP*, October 2, 2017.

61 Florian Rötzer: "USA lehnen Zusatzprotokoll zur Biowaffenkonvention ab" ("US Rejects Additional Protocol to Biological Weapons Convention"), *Telepolis*, July 23, 2001.

62 Bundeszentrale für politische Bildung (German Federal Agency for Civic Education), Bonn International Center for Conversion: "Verbot ohne Überprüfung—die Biowaffenkonvention (BWK) und ihre Lücken" ("Prohibition without Verification—The Biological Weapons Convention and its Gaps"), November 2013.

63 Dwight D. Eisenhower: "Farewell Radio and Television Address to the American People," January 17, 1961. Excerpt: "In the councils of government, we must guard against the acquisition of unwarranted influence, whether sought or unsought, by the military-industrial complex. The potential for the disastrous rise of misplaced power exists and will persist. We must never let the weight of this combination endanger our liberties or democratic processes."

64 Michael Hennes: "Der neue Militärisch-Industrielle Komplex in den USA" ("The New Military-Industrial Complex in the United States"), Bundeszentrale für politische Bildung, *Aus Politik und Zeitgeschichte* (German Federal Agency for Civic Education, *Politics and Contemporary History*), Issue 46/2003, pp. 41–46, November 5, 2003.

65 Fred Kaplan, "Powell: The U.S. Is 'Running Out Of Demons,'" *Boston Globe*, April 9, 1991.

66 "A National Security Strategy of Engagement and Enlargement," The White House, July 1994.

67 US Senate: "Omnibus Counterterrorism Act of 1995," February 10, 1995.

68 Neil A. Lewis: "Anti-Terrorism Bill: Blast Turns a Snail Into a Race Horse," *New York Times*, April 21, 1995.

69 Jo Thomas: "McVeigh Letters Before Blast Show the Depth of His Anger," *New York Times*, July 1, 1998; Wendy S. Painting: "Aberration in the Heartland of the Real: The Secret Lives of Timothy McVeigh," Trine Day, 2016. Author Wendy S. Painting reports in her book that a few days after the attack, McVeigh described to his originally assigned attorneys, John Coyle and Susan Otto, that he had been recruited to work undercover in the military by a major he knew from his deployment in the Gulf War (this information was not disclosed to the public at the time, and was only later found in the files). He was supposed to infiltrate neo-Nazi and other terrorist groups. He said that in the course of this undercover work he learned of plans for the bombing and was instructed by his commanding officer to cooperate in the plot, ensuring that only a few windows in the building would be broken. McVeigh explained to attorneys his shock after seeing the scale of the attack, suggesting someone had switched either the truck or the explosives inside at the last minute without his knowledge. Later, McVeigh changed his story several times. Most recently, shortly before his execution in 2001, he retold it to fellow inmate David Paul Hammer, who recounted it in a book. According to Hammer, McVeigh believed in the last days of his life that his commanding officer would save him from execution at the last minute by having him fake the killing (by lethal injection), after which he could start a new life.

70 Presidential Decision Directive/NSC-39, The White House, June 21, 1995.

71 Joseph Nye, James Woolsey: "Defend Against the Shadow Enemy," *Los Angeles Times*, June 1, 1997.

72 Judith Miller, William J. Broad, Stephen Engelberg: "Germs: Biological Weapons and America's Secret War," Simon & Schuster, 2001, p. 216.

73 Michael Crowley: "Long Shot," *The New Republic*, November 5, 2001.

74 Eric Lipton: "Doubts Persist Among Anthrax Suspect's Colleagues," *New York Times*, August 8, 2008. Excerpt: "The vaccine controversy erupted in the late 1990s, after the Defense Department ordered the inoculation of all 2.4 million active duty and reserve troops, starting with those most likely to confront biological attacks in war zones, partly because Iraq had confirmed that it once had a large stockpile of anthrax that was destroyed after the first Persian Gulf war. By 2000, more than 570,000 military personnel had complied with the order, and hundreds had filed an 'adverse event report' after receiving the shots, citing reactions that included fatigue, dizziness and muscle pain, and more serious conditions like thyroid disorders and rhabdomyolysis, a muscle ailment. Congressional hearings were held, and dozens of House members signed a letter to the Pentagon calling the mandatory vaccination program 'a flawed policy that should be immediately stopped.'"

75 Maureen Dowd: "Liberties; Anthrax, Shmanthrax," *New York Times*, November 19, 1997.

76 Judith Miller, Stephen Engelberg, William J. Broad: "U.S. Germ Warfare Research Pushes Treaty Limits," *New York Times*, September 4, 2001.

77 Judith Miller, William J. Broad, Stephen Engelberg: "Germs: Biological Weapons and America's Secret War," Simon & Schuster, 2001, p. 383f.

78 US Department of Defense: News Briefing, Victoria Clarke, September 4, 2001.

79 Judith Miller, William J. Broad: "Exercise Finds U.S. Unable to Handle Germ War Threat," *New York Times*, April 26, 1998.

80 Ibid.

81 Madeline Baro: "FBI: 3 Plotted To Kill Clinton," *AP*, July 16, 1998.

82 Presidential Decision Directives 62 und 63, The White House, May 22, 1998.

83 Project for the New American Century: "Statement of Principles," June 3, 1997.

84 Project for the New American Century: "Letter to President Clinton on Iraq," January 26, 1998.

85 "Scott Ritter on the Untold Story of the Intelligence Conspiracy to Undermine the UN and Overthrow Saddam Hussein," *Democracy Now*, October 21, 2005.

86 Josh Rogin: "Giselle Donnelly can finally be herself," *Washington Post*, October 12, 2018.

87 Project for the New American Century: "Rebuilding America's Defenses," p. 51.

88 Ibid. p, 60.

89 Lt. Col. Robert P. Kadlec: "Twenty-First Century Germ Warfare," in: Barry R. Schneider, Lawrence E. Grinter: "Battlefield of the Future—21st Century Warfare Issues," Studies in National Security No. 3, Air War College, September 1995, Revised Edition, September 1998, p. 228, 248. I would like to thank my colleague Dirk Pohlmann for referring me to this document.

90 Charles Davis: "Robert Kadlec, the Trump administration's top official for addressing biological threats, awarded a $2 billion contract to a company he used to advise," *Business Insider*, May 5, 2020.

91 Raul Diego, Whitney Webb: "Head of the Hydra: The Rise of Robert Kadlec," *Mintpress*, May 15, 2020.

DARK WINTER: A STATE OF EMERGENCY IS TESTED (1998–2001)

92 Gigi Kwik Gronvall: "Preparing for Bioterrorism: The Sloan Foundation's Leadership in Biosecurity," Center for Biosecurity of UPMC, 2012.

93 Edwin Black: "Nazis rode to war on GM wheels," *San Francisco Chronicle*, January 7, 2007.

94 Matthias Holland-Letz: "Scheinheilige Stifter: Wie Reiche und Unternehmen durch gemeinnützige Stiftungen noch mächtiger werden" ("Hypocritical philanthropists: how the rich and corporations are becoming even more powerful through charitable foundations"), Backstein Verlag, 2015.

95 US Senate: Nominations—Hearings before the Committee on Armed Services, 83rd Congress, 1st Session on Nominee Designates, January 15, 1953.

96 National Symposium on Medical and Public Health—Response to Bioterrorism: The Foundation for Coordinating a Strategic Response, February 16–17, 1999, Arlington, Virginia.

97 Richard A. Clarke: "Finding the Right Balance against Bioterrorism," *Emerging Infectious Diseases*, Vol. 5, No. 4, August 1999, p. 497.

98 Colonel Gerald W. Parker: "Potential Biological Weapons Threats," *Emerging Infectious Diseases*, Vol. 5, No. 4, August 1999, pp. 523–527.

99 Judith Miller, Stephen Engelberg, William J. Broad: "U.S. Germ Warfare Research Pushes Treaty Limits," *New York Times*, September 4, 2001.

100 Tara O'Toole: "Smallpox: An Attack Scenario," *Emerging Infectious Diseases*, Vol. 5, No. 4, August 1999, pp. 540–546.

101 Jason Bardi: "Aftermath of a Hypothetical Smallpox Disaster," *Emerging Infectious Diseases*, Vol. 5, No. 4, August 1999, pp. 547–551.

102 Tara O'Toole: "Smallpox: An Attack Scenario," *Emerging Infectious Diseases*, Vol. 5, No. 4, August 1999, p. 546.

103 Second National Symposium on Medical and Public Health Response to Bioterrorism, November 28–29, 2000, Washington.

104 D. A. Henderson: "Welcome and Symposium Introduction," *Public Health Reports*, 2001 Suppl. 2, Vol. 116, p. 1.

105 Tara O'Toole, Thomas Inglesby: "Epidemic Response Scenario: Decision Making in a Time of Plague," *Public Health Reports*, 2001 Suppl. 2, Vol. 116, pp. 92–103.

106 Ibid. p. 100.

107 Ibid.

108 Ibid.

109 Ibid. p. 101.

110 Konrad Lischka: "In öffentlicher Mission" ("On a public mission"), *Der Spiegel*, October 23, 2000; Bernd Kling: "In-Q-Tel: Interessenkonflikte bei CIA-Investitionen im Silicon Valley" ("In-Q-Tel: Conflicts of interest in CIA investments in Silicon Valley"), *ZDNet*, September 1, 2016.

111 Tara O'Toole, Michael Mair, Thomas V. Inglesby: "Shining Light on 'Dark Winter,'" *Clinical Infectious Diseases*, Vol. 34, Issue 7, April 1, 2002, pp. 972–983.

112 Dark Winter, Bioterrorism Exercise, Andrews Air Force Base, June 22–23, 2001, Final Script, p. 34, centerforhealthsecurity.org/our-work/events-archive/2001_dark-winter/Dark Winter Script.pdf

113 Tara O'Toole, Michael Mair, Thomas V. Inglesby: "Shining Light on 'Dark Winter,'" *Clinical Infectious Diseases*, Vol. 34, Issue 7, April 1, 2002, pp. 972–983.

114 Dark Winter, Bioterrorism Exercise, Andrews Air Force Base, June 22–23, 2001, Final Script, p. 40.

115 Tara O'Toole, Michael Mair, Thomas V. Inglesby: "Shining Light on 'Dark Winter,'" *Clinical Infectious Diseases*, Vol. 34, Issue 7, April 1, 2002, pp. 972–983.

116 Dark Winter, Bioterrorism Exercise, Andrews Air Force Base, June 22–23, 2001, Final Script, p. 39.

117 Dana Priest: "CIA Holds Terror Suspects in Secret Prisons," *Washington Post*, November 1, 2005; "Nur die Spitze des Eisbergs" ("Just the Tip of the Iceberg"), Amnesty International, January 9, 2009.

118 Florian Rötzer: "Bundesgericht weist Teile des Patriot Act als verfassungswidrig zurück" ("Federal Court Rejects Parts of the Patriot Act as Unconstitutional"), *Telepolis*, September 27, 2007.

119 John Lancaster: "Anti Terrorism Bill Hits Snag on the Hill: Dispute Between Senate Democrats, White House Threatens Committee Approval," *Washington Post*, October 3, 2001; John Lancaster: "Senate Reaches Deal On Anti-Terror Bill," *Washington Post*, October 4, 2001.

120 Anthony York: "Why Daschle and Leahy?" *Salon.com*, November 21 2001. Excerpt: "It's the question no one in Washington or the media wants to publicly examine: Why were two high-profile Democrats targeted by the anthrax mail terrorist? ... Leahy is also an unabashed liberal, who led the charge against President Bush's most conservative Cabinet nominees, including Solicitor General Theodore Olson and Attorney General John Ashcroft. The senator from Vermont has also been one of the president's most outspoken critics since Sept. 11, as the administration has moved aggressively to curtail civil liberties in its war on terrorism."

121 "Bush asks Daschle to limit Sept. 11 probes," CNN, January 29, 2002. Excerpt: "'The vice president expressed the concern that a review of what happened on September 11 would take resources and personnel away from the effort in the war on terrorism,' Daschle told reporters."

122 Scott Shane: "Colleague Disputes Case Against Anthrax Suspect," *New York Times*, April 22, 2010; Glenn Greenwald: "Serious doubt cast on FBI's anthrax case against Bruce Ivins," *Salon.com*, February 16, 2011.

123 Graeme MacQueen: "The 2001 Anthrax Deception. The Case for a Domestic Conspiracy," Clarity Press, 2014.

124 Eric Lipton: "Doubts Persist Among Anthrax Suspect's Colleagues," *New York Times*, August 8, 2008.

125 Ibid.

126 Carsten Volkery: "Der Impfstoffskandal" ("The Vaccine Scandal"), *Der Spiegel*, October 17, 2001.

127 BioPort: "BioPort Corporation gains FDA approval," January 31, 2002. Excerpt: "Robert Kramer, President of BioPort Corporation, today announced the company has cleared its final Food and Drug Administration hurdle—allowing the distribution of anthrax vaccine from its renovated facility. BioPort had received tentative approval from the FDA in December of 2001."

ATLANTIC STORM: EPIDEMICS AS DOOR OPENERS (2001-2018)

128 "Acambis and Baxter land $428 million smallpox vaccine deal with US govt," *The Pharma Letter*, November 30, 2001.

129 Naomi Aoki: "Transformation of Acambis," *Boston Globe*, April 16, 2003.

130 One Health Commission, Biography Thomas P. Monath, February 2015, https://www.onehealthcommission.org/documents/filelibrary/events_and_calendar/oh_day/coord_team_bios/Tom_Monath_Biography_January2014_20_D823B769A51B4.pdf

131 Michael Hilbig: "Gefährliches Ministerium" ("Dangerous Ministry"), *Focus*, No. 9/2003, February 24, 2003.

132 Gerhard Piper: "ABC-Abwehr: Präventiveinsätze der Bundeswehr im Innern?" ("NBC Defense: Preventive Missions of the German Federal Army in the Interior?"), *antimilitarismus information*, ami No. 5/6, 2003.

133 Philip Bethge, Georg Mascolo: "Masterplan gegen Killerviren" ("Masterplan against Killer Viruses"), *Der Spiegel*, Nr. 3/2003, January 13, 2003.

134 Esther Kogelboom: "Gemeinsam gegen Pocken" ("Together against Smallpox"), *Der Tagesspiegel*, November 8, 2003.

135 "Move to share bio-terrorism fight," BBC News, November 8, 2001.

136 Website of the Global Health Security Initiative, ghsi.ca/about/. Excerpt: "Following the terrorist attacks on September 11, 2001, former United States Secretary of Health and Human Services Tommy Thompson suggested that countries fighting bioterrorism should meet to share information and coordinate their efforts to improve global health security."

137 "Health Ministers Take Action to Improve Health Security Globally," Global Health Security Initiative, Ministerial Statement, November 7, 2001, Ottawa, Canada.

138 Ibid.

139 "Health Ministers Launch Initiatives to Improve Health Security Globally," Global Health Security Initiative, Ministerial Statement, December 6, 2002, Mexico City.

140 Exercise Global Mercury, Post Exercise Report, January 12, 2005, p. 13, https://www.rki.de/EN/Content/infections/biological/Preparedness_Plan/Exercise.pdf?__blob=publicationFile

141 Ibid., p. 18.

142 Ibid., p. 10.

143 Atlantic Storm website, centerforhealthsecurity.org/our-work/events-archive/2005_atlantic_storm/

144 Atlantic Storm website, About Atlantic Storm, Trial Run Participants, https://web.archive.org/web/20060902020706/atlanticstorm.org/about/participants.html

145 Bradley T. Smith et al.: "Navigating the Storm: Report and Recommendations from the Atlantic Storm Exercise," *Biosecurity and Bioterrorism*, Vol. 3, No. 3, 2005, p. 261.

146 Kathrin Gießelmann: "Walter Biederbick: Gesundheit im internationalen Kontext stärken" ("Walter Biederbick: Strengthening Health in an International Context"), *Deutsches Ärzteblatt*, Issue 7/2019, February 15, 2019; web.archive.org/web/20050924034056/http://www.atlanticstorm.org/about/observers.html

147 Atlantic Storm website, About the Transatlantic Biosecurity Network, centerforhealthsecurity.org/our-work/events-archive/2005_atlantic_storm/transatlantic-network.html

148 Robert Koch Institute: "RKI 2010—eine Zwischenbilanz. Der Ausbau des Robert Koch-Instituts zu einem Public Health Institut für Deutschland" ("RKI 2010—An Interim Assessment. The Expansion of the Robert Koch Institute into a Public Health Institute for Germany"), 2009, p. 18. This 2009 publication also stated that "the press officers of the responsible federal and state institutions [were] involved in the pandemic communication concept." It went on to prophetically state that Biederbick believed that "the public media would also presumably cooperate closely with government agencies during an influenza pandemic."

149 Bradley T. Smith et al.: "Navigating the Storm: Report and Recommendations from the Atlantic Storm Exercise," *Biosecurity and Bioterrorism*, Vol. 3, No. 3, 2005, p. 256–267, centerforhealthsecurity.org/our-work/events-archive/2005_atlantic_storm/pdf/Atlantic Storm After-Action.pdf; Atlantic Storm website, About Atlantic Storm, Overview of Exercise, web.archive.org/web/20050404063955/http://www.atlantic-storm.org/about/overview.html

150 Thomas Kleine-Brockhoff: "Wenn die Pocken kommen" ("When the Smallpox Comes"), *Die Zeit*, January 27, 2005.

151 Bradley T. Smith et al.: "Navigating the Storm: Report and Recommendations from the Atlantic Storm Exercise," *Biosecurity and Bioterrorism*, Vol. 3, No. 3, 2005, p. 258.

152 Atlantic Storm, Guide for Viewers and Facilitators, 2006, p. 6, centerforhealthsecurity.org/our-work/events-archive/2005_atlantic_storm/pdf/as_Interactive_guide.pdf

153 Bradley T. Smith et al.: "Navigating the Storm: Report and Recommendations from the Atlantic Storm Exercise," *Biosecurity and Bioterrorism*, Vol. 3, No. 3, 2005, p. 263.

154 WHO: "Cumulative number of confirmed human cases for avian influenza A(H5N1) reported to WHO, 2003–2009," November 25, 2019.

155 The quotes in this paragraph are from: "President Outlines Pandemic Influenza Preparations and Response," The White House, November 1, 2005.

156 Nelson D. Schwartz: "Rumsfeld's growing stake in Tamiflu," CNN, October 31, 2005.

157 "Laut Weltgesundheitsorganisation erreicht Vogelgrippe beispielloses Ausmaß" ("World Health Organization says bird flu reaches unprecedented levels"), European Commission, January 27, 2004.

158 Klaus Remme: "WHO-Sprecher warnt vor Übergreifen der Vogelgrippe auf Deutschland" ("WHO spokesman warns of bird flu spread to Germany"), *Deutschlandfunk*, October 14, 2005.

159 WHO, Department of Communicable Disease, Surveillance and Response, "WHO Guidelines on the Use of Vaccines and Antivirals during Influenza Pandemics," 2004.

160 Rüdiger Meyer: "Tamiflu: Eine unendliche Geschichte um Datentransparenz" ("Tamiflu: A never-ending story about data transparency"), *Deutsches Ärzteblatt*, Issue 4/2013, January 25, 2013.

161 Deutscher Bundestag, Plenarprotokoll (German parliament, Plenary Minutes), 16/10, January 18, 2006, dip21.bundestag.de/dip21/btp/16/16010.pdf

162 Nicola Kuhrt: "Deutschland zahlte 330 millionen Euro für fragwürdige Grippemittel" ("Germany paid 330 million euros for questionable flu medication"), *Der Spiegel*, February 14, 2015.

163 Jim McElhatton: "Obama nominee omitted ties to biotech," *Washington Times*, September 8, 2009.

164 Ibid.

165 Johns Hopkins Center for Health Security, Professional Profile Anita Cicero, centerforhealthsecurity.org/our-people/cicero/

166 Center for Biosecurity, Professional Profile Anita Cicero, Chief Operating Officer and Deputy Director, upmc-biosecurity.org/website/our_staff/cicero.html

167 "Scenarios for the Future of Technology and International Development," Rockefeller Foundation, May 2010, p. 18ff, web.archive.org/web/20100701154450/http://www.rockefellerfoundation.org/uploads/files/bba493f7-cc97-4da3-add6-3deb007cc719.pdf

168 Ibid., p. 19.

169 Ibid., p. 6.

170 Norbert Häring: "Gleichschritt—Das unheimlich weitsichtige Pandemie-Szenario der Rockefeller Stiftung" ("Lockstep—The Rockefeller Foundation's Uncannily Far-Sighted Pandemic Scenario"), norberthaering.de, May 12, 2020.

171 Michaela Wiegel: "Der unergründliche Monsieur Macron" ("The unfathomable Monsieur Macron"), FAZ.net, May 6, 2017.

172 Jacques Attali: "Changer, par précaution" ("Change, as a precaution"), L'Express, May 3, 2009, blogs.lexpress.fr/attali/2009/05/03/changer_par_precaution/

173 "Improving Epidemic Response: Building Bridges Between the US and China," Center for Biosecurity, May 15, 2012, Washington.

174 US CDC in China website, cdc.gov/globalhealth/countries/china/pdf/china.factsheet_from_china_office_cleared.pdf

175 Ibid.

176 US CDC in China, 2010–2011 Annual Report, p. 25, cdc.gov/globalhealth/countries/china/pdF/us_china-biennial-report_2010-11.pdf

177 Ibid., p. 24.

CLADE X: A BIOWEAPON FOR POPULATION REDUCTION (2018)

178 Katrin Elger, Jens Glüsing, Markus Grill, Veronika Hackenbroch, Jan Puhl, Mathieu von Rohr, Gerald Traufetter: "Rekonstruktion des Schweinegrippe-Debakels—Die Pandemie, die keine war" ("Reconstructing the Swine Flu Debacle—The Pandemic That Wasn't a Pandemic"), Der Spiegel, June 11, 2020.

179 Alyson Shontell: "Bill Gates warnt vor einer neuen Art Terrorismus: 'Ihr Zerstörungspotential ist s ehr groß'" ("Bill Gates warns of a new kind of terrorism: 'Its destructive potential is great'"), Business Insider, January 20, 2017.

180 Clive Cookson, Tim Bradshaw: "Davos launch for coalition to prevent epidemics of emerging viruses," Financial Times, January 18, 2017.

181 Ibid. Excerpt: "'If we can't get it under a year we'd be disappointed,' Mr Gates told the FT in an interview at the World Economic Forum in Davos. ... Targets include six viruses with known potential to cause serious epidemics: Mers, Lassa, Nipah, Ebola, Marburg and Zika. But an equally important part of the programme will be to build the scientific and technological infrastructure for developing vaccines quickly against pathogens that emerge from nowhere to cause a global health crisis, such as Sars in 2002/03 and Zika in 2015/16."

182 Mathias Müller von Blumencron: "Der Westen in Therapie" ("The West in Therapy"), FAZ, February 18, 2017.

183 John McCain: "McCain Opening Remarks at Munich Security Conference," February 17, 2017, youtube.com/watch?v=TNeLmjuMtIU

184 Munich Security Conference 2017: "Speech by Bill Gates at the 53rd Munich Security Conference," February 18, 2017.

185 Crystal Watson et al.: "Clade X: A Pandemic Exercise," Health Security, Vol. 17, No. 5, October 7, 2019, S. 412, liebertpub.com/doi/pdf/10.1089/hs.2019.0097

186 Ben Hirschler: "U.S. biotechs to speed work on Nipah vaccine as virus hits India," Reuters, May 24, 2018; Jestin Abraham: "Silently, additional chief secretary Rajeev Sadanandan gained the ammo to take on Nipah," The New Indian Express, June 10, 2018.

187 Center for Health Security, Clade X website, Resources, Background Materials, "Clade X Background: A Brigher Dawn," centerforhealthsecurity.org/our-work/events/2018_clade_x_exercise/pdfs/Clade-X-A-Brighter-Dawn-Background.pdf

188 The participants included: Secretary of State: John Bellinger, former Legal Adviser for the US Department of State and the National Security Council; Secretary of Defense: James Talent, former US Senator; Attorney General: Jamie Gorelick, former Deputy Attorney General of the United States, Commissioner on the 9/11 Commission; Secretary of Health and Human Services: Margaret (Peggy) Hamburg, former Commissioner of the FDA, former Commissioner of the New York City Department of Health and Mental Hygiene; Secretary of Homeland Security: Tara O'Toole, Executive Vice President and Senior Fellow, In-Q-Tel, former Under Secretary for Science and Technology; CIA Director: Jeffrey Smith, former General Counsel of the CIA; Senate Majority Leader: Tom Daschle, former US Senator, Senate Majority Leader; Speaker of the House of Representatives: Susan Brooks, Congresswoman, former US Attorney for the Southern District of Indiana; CDC Director: Julie Gerberding, former CDC Director.

189 Center for Health Security, Clade X website, Resources, Clade X Exercise Presentation Slides, p. 11, centerforhealthsecurity.org/our-work/events/2018_clade_x_exercise/pdfs/Clade-X-exercise-presentation-slides.pdf

190 Ibid., p. 31.

191 Crystal Watson et al.: "Clade X: A Pandemic Exercise," Health Security, Vol. 17, No. 5, October 7, 2019, p. 415.

192 Ibid., p. 414.

193 Vera Zylka Menhorn, Dustin Grunert: "Genbasierte Impfstoffe: Hoffnungsträger auch zum Schutz vor SARS-CoV-2" ("Gene-based vaccines: Hope for protection against SARS-CoV-2"), Deutsches Ärzteblatt, Ausgabe 21/2020, May 22, 2020.

194 Center for Health Security, Clade X website, Resources, Implications of Clade X for National Policy, p. 1.

195 Crystal Watson et al.: "Clade X: A Pandemic Exercise," Health Security, Vol. 17, No. 5, October 7, 2019, p. 417.

196 Dustin Moskovitz: "Compelled to Act," Medium, September 9, 2016.

197 Open Philanthropy website, Focus Areas, Biosecurity and Pandemic Preparedness, openphilanthropy.org/focus/global-catastrophic-risks/biosecurity

198 Theodore Schleifer: "Facebook co-founder Dustin Moskovitz commits $20M to help beat Trump," CNN, September 9, 2016.

199 Dustin Moskovitz: "Compelled to Act," Medium, September 9, 2016.

200 Ibid.

EVENT 201: CORONAVIRUS CRISIS AS A SIMULATION GAME (2019)

201 Website of the WEF, https://web.archive.org/web/20200501030900/weforum.org/about/our-members-and-partners

202 Website of the WEF, https://web.archive.org/web/20210128161247/https://www.weforum.org/about/what-makes-us-unique

203 Website of the WEF, https://web.archive.org/web/20200511115252/https://www.weforum.org/about/strategic-partners

204 Event 201 website, centerforhealthsecurity.org/event201/about

205 Event 201 website, The Event 201 Scenario, centerforhealthsecurity.org/event201/scenario.html

206 Event 201 website, Players, centerforhealthsecurity.org/event201/players/index.html

207 Kyle O'Brien: "Edelman COO Matthew Harrington elevated to global president," *The Drum*, October 1, 2019.

208 Lee Fang: "Former Obama Officials Help Silicon Valley Pitch the Pentagon for Lucrative Defense Contracts," *The Intercept*, July 22, 2018.

209 Michael Fumento: "Why The WHO Faked A Pandemic," *Forbes*, February 5, 2010; Katrin Elger, Jens Glüsing, Markus Grill, Veronika Hackenbroch, Jan Puhl, Mathieu von Rohr, Gerald Traufetter: "Rekonstruktion des Schweinegrippe-Debakels—Die Pandemie, die keine war" ("Reconstructing the Swine Flu Debacle—The Pandemic That Wasn't a Pandemic"), *Der Spiegel*, June 11, 2020.

210 Event 201 website, Players, Stephen C Redd, centerforhealthsecurity.org/event201/players/redd.html

211 Michael D. Shear et al.: "The Lost Month: How a Failure to Test Blinded the U.S. to Covid-19," *New York Times*, March 28, 2020.

212 Na Zhu et al.: "A Novel Coronavirus from Patients with Pneumonia in China, 2019," *New England Journal of Medicine*, January 24, 2020; Chen Wang et al.: "A novel coronavirus outbreak of global health concern," *The Lancet*, January 24, 2020.

213 Johns Hopkins Center for Health Security: "Event 201 Pandemic Exercise: Segment 1, Intro and Medical Countermeasures (MCM) Discussion," November 4, 2019, video (min. 55), youtube.com/watch?v=Vm1-DnxRiPM

214 Johns Hopkins Center for Health Security: "Event 201 Pandemic Exercise: Segment 4, Communications Discussion and Epilogue Video," November 4, 2019, youtube.com/watch?v=LBuP40H4Tko

215 Ibid., min. 10.

216 Ibid., min. 19.

217 Ibid., min. 20.

218 Ibid., min. 25.

219 Event 201 website, Event 201 Recommendations: "Public-private cooperation for pandemic preparedness and response—A call to action," centerforhealthsecurity.org/event201/recommendations.html

220 centerforhealthsecurity.org/event201/videos.html

221 Shawn McCarthy: "Ted Turner urges global one-child policy to save planet," *The Globe and Mail*, December 5, 2010.

EXCURSUS: POPULATION CONTROL

222 The World Bank website, Reproductive, Maternal, Newborn, Child, and Adolescent Health, at April 2, 2020, worldbank.org/en/topic/reproductivematernalchildhealth

223 demographicdividend.org

224 World Bank Group: "Achieving the Demographic Dividend: An Operational Tool for Country-Specific Investment Decision-Making in Pre-Dividend Countries," January 1, 2019.

225 Urs Hafner: "'Überzählig sind immer die Anderen'–Die Anthropologin Shalini Randeria über die Aporien der Bevölkerungspolitik" ("'Supernumerary are always the others'–Anthropologist Shalini Randeria on the aporias of population policy"), Neue Zürcher Zeitung, April 29, 2013.

226 Joseph Stiglitz: "Globalization and Its Discontents," W.W. Norton & Company, 2002.

227 Naomi Klein: "The Shock Doctrine," Knopf Canada, 2007.

228 Jean Ziegler: "Wir lassen sie verhungern: Die Massenvernichtung in der Dritten Welt" ("We are letting them starve: mass destruction in the Third World"), Bertelsmann, 2012.

229 John Pilger: "Hidden Agendas," Vintage, 1998.

230 Michel Chossudovsky: "The Globalization of Poverty and the New World Order," Global Research, 2003.

231 Population Council website, popcouncil.org/about/product-licensing

232 Joan Dunlop: "John D. Rockefeller 3rd, Statesman and Founder of the Population Council," Population Today, September 1, 2000. The author, Joan Dunlop, a women's rights activist and daughter of the vice chairman of the oil company BP, was Rockefeller's personal advisor at the time.

233 McNamara describes it himself on camera in the 2003 documentary "The Fog of War" by Errol Morris.

234 World Bank Group Archives Holdings: Records of the Population, Health, and Nutrition Sector, July 30, 2012. Excerpt: "Functional responsibility for population-related activities was first articulated in the organizational structure of the World Bank after the November 1, 1968 reorganization of the Projects Department (PRJ). ... The Bank's first population loan was made to Jamaica in 1970. This and subsequent loans: supported services related to population management; created awareness of and provided information about population issues; and devised and implemented incentives and disincentives aimed at encouraging smaller families."

235 The World Bank is traditionally headed by an American. The US also holds the most voting rights over any other country in the World Bank by a wide margin, in line with its financial commitment. worldbank.org/en/about/leadership/votingpowers

236 National Security Study Memorandum NSSM 200, Implications of Worldwide Population Growth For U.S. Security and Overseas Interests, December 10, 1974, p. 58, 65, pdf.usaid.gov/pdf_docs/PCAAB500.pdf

237 Memorandum NSC-U/DM-130A From the Chairman of the National Security Council Under Secretaries Committee (Robinson) to President Ford, July 29, 1976, Attachment: U.S. International Population Policy: First Annual Report, prepared by the Interagency Task Force on Population Policy, May 1976, history.state.gov/historicaldocuments/frus1969-76ve14p1/d125

238 Hearings before the Select Committee on Population, 95th Congress, 2nd Session, March 7–9, 1978: Fertility and Contraception in America, Contraceptive Technology and Development, p. 340ff.

239 Eric Wagner: "Der Impfaktivismus der Gates-Stiftung" ("The Gates Foundation's Vaccination Activism"), Multipolar, April 16, 2020; John W. Oller et al.: "HCG Found in WHO Tetanus Vaccine in Kenya Raises Concern in the Developing World," Open Access Library Journal, Vol. 4, No. 10, October 27, 2017.

240 Tim Evans: "An Optimist's View of Global Health Achievement," Rockefeller Foundation, January 26, 2013.

241 Zunaid Ahmed Palak: "How digital inclusion made Bangladesh a standout South Asian economy," World Economic Forum, February 26, 2020.

242 id2020.org

243 Chris Burt: "ID2020 and partners launch program to provide digital ID with vaccines," *Biometric Update*, September 20, 2019.

244 Norbert Häring: "ID2020, Known-Traveller und Kontaktverfolgung durch Google und Apple: US-Konzerne werden zur Weltpassbehörde" ("ID2020, Known-Traveler and Contact Tracing by Google and Apple: US Corporations Become World Passport Agencies"), *norberthaering.de*, April 16, 2020.

IMPENDING COLLAPSE: THE SEPTEMBER 2019 FINANCIAL MARKETS QUAKE

245 Heike Buchter: "Kurzschluss im Finanzsystem" ("Short Circuit in the Financial System"), *Die Zeit*, October 1, 2019.

246 Board of Governors of the Federal Reserve System, Credit and Liquidity Programs and the Balance Sheet, Recent balance sheet trends, https://www.federalreserve.gov/monetarypolicy/bst_recenttrends.htm

247 Ibid.

248 Jeff Cox: "The Fed is looking at a 'standing repo' operation to handle overnight funding issues," CNBC, November 20, 2019.

249 Norbert Häring: "Die US-Notenbank subventioniert mit billigen Notkrediten Mega-Gewinne der Großbanken" ("Fed subsidizes big banks' mega-profits with cheap emergency loans"), *Geld und mehr*, January 16, 2020.

250 Pam Martens, Russ Martens: "Wall Street's Financial Crisis Preceded COVID-19: Chart and Timeline," Wall Street on Parade, May 1, 2020.

COVID IN DAVOS: A VIRUS IS INTRODUCED (JANUARY 2020)

251 "Mysteriöse Lungenkrankheit in Zentralchina ausgebrochen" ("Mysterious lung disease outbreak in central China"), *dpa*, December 31, 2019.

252 "Chinese officials investigate cause of pneumonia outbreak in Wuhan," *Reuters*, December 31, 2019.

253 "Wuhan Municipal Health Commission on the current situation of pneumonia in our city," December 31, 2019, web.archive.org/web/20200109215413/http://wjw.wuhan.gov.cn/front/web/showDetail/2019123108989

254 "8 people spread false information about pneumonia and were prosecuted," *Chutian Dushi Bao*, January 1, 2020; "Mysteriöse Lungenkrankheit in China ausgebrochen" ("Mysterious lung disease outbreak in China"), *Welt*, January 1, 2020.

255 Josh Margolin, James Gordon Meek: "Intelligence report warned of coronavirus crisis as early as November: Sources," *ABC News*, April 9, 2020; "US alerted Israel, NATO to disease outbreak in China in November—TV report," *The Times of Israel*, April 16, 2020.

256 Steffen Wurzel: "Neuer Virustyp entdeckt" ("New type of virus discovered"), *tagesschau.de*, January 9, 2020.

257 "Erster Test für das neuartige Coronavirus in China ist entwickelt" ("First test for novel coronavirus in China is developed"), press release of the Deutschen Zentrums für Infektionsforschung (German Center for Infection Research), January 16, 2020.

258 Volkart Wildermuth: "Diagnostischer Test aus Berlin weltweit gefragt" ("Diagnostic Test from Berlin in Demand Worldwide"), *Deutschlandfunk*, January 23, 2020.

259 Johns Hopkins Center for Health Security: "The Johns Hopkins Center for Health Security, World Economic Forum, and Bill & Melinda Gates Foundation Call for Public-Private Cooperation for Pandemic Preparedness and Response," January 17, 2020.

260 China CDC: "Tracking the Epidemic," weekly.chinacdc.cn/news/TrackingtheEpidemic.htm

261 The 8 p.m. edition of the German television news program *Tagesschau*, January 20, 2020.

262 WHO: "Novel Coronavirus (2019-nCoV) Situation Report-1," January 21, 2020.

263 Laura Santhanam: "Track the spread of novel coronavirus with this map," PBS Newshour, Jan. 22, 2020.

264 WHO: "Statement on the meeting of the International Health Regulations (2005) Emergency Committee regarding the outbreak of novel coronavirus (2019-nCoV)," January 23, 2013. Excerpt: "On 22 January, the members of the Emergency Committee expressed divergent views on whether this event constitutes a PHEIC or not. At that time, the advice was that the event did not constitute a PHEIC, but the Committee members agreed on the urgency of the situation and suggested that the Committee should be reconvened in a matter of days to examine the situation further."

265 "Fears Over New Coronavirus Grip Davos"; "How China's Virus Outbreak Could Threaten the Global Economy," *New York Times*, January 23, 2020.

266 Bradley T. Smith et al.: "Navigating the Storm: Report and Recommendations from the Atlantic Storm Exercise," *Biosecurity and Bioterrorism*, Vol. 3, No. 3, 2005, pp. 256–267.

267 David Yanofsky: "The confidential list of everyone attending the 2020 World Economic Forum in Davos," *Quartz*, January 21, 2020.

268 "EU bestellt bei AstraZeneca Corona-Impfstoff in großem Stil" ("EU orders Coronavirus vaccine from AstraZeneca in bulk"), *boerse.ARD.de*, June 14, 2020.

269 André Anwar: "Richard Hatchett—der Herr über die Corona-Impfstoffe" ("Richard Hatchett—master of coronavirus vaccines"), *RND*, March 17, 2020.

270 David Yanofsky: "The confidential list of everyone attending the 2020 World Economic Forum in Davos," *Quartz*, January 21, 2020.

271 Saad B. Omer: "Is America Ready for Another Outbreak?—No. But there are clear steps the government needs to take," *New York Times*, January 23, 2020.

272 WHO: "Novel Coronavirus (2019-nCoV) Situation Report-4," January 24, 2020.

273 China CDC: "Tracking the Epidemic," weekly.chinacdc.cn/news/TrackingtheEpidemic.htm

274 Ibid.

275 Victoria Taft: "Report: China Stopped Testing for COVID-19. That's Why There Are Zero New Cases," *PJ Media*, March 21, 2020.

276 WHO: "Report of the WHO-China Joint Mission on Coronavirus Disease 2019 (COVID-19)," February 28, 2020, p. 17, who.int/docs/default-source/coronaviruse/who-china-joint-mission-on-covid-19-final-report.pdf. Excerpt: "Several sources of data support this conclusion, including the steep decline in fever clinic visits, the opening up of treatment beds as cured patients are discharged, and the challenges to recruiting new patients for clinical trials. Based on a comparison of crude attack rates across provinces, the Joint Mission estimates that this truly all-of-Government and all-of-society approach that has been taken in China has averted or at least delayed hundreds of thousands of COVID-19 cases in the country."

DEATHS IN EUROPE: PANIC AND DECEPTION (FEBRUARY 2020)

277 Michael Meyen: "Breaking News. Die Welt im Ausnahmezustand" ("Breaking News. The World in a State of Emergency"), Westend, 2018.

278 The 8 p.m. edition of the German news program *Tagesschau*, February 24, 2020.

279 Press conference by Jens Spahn at the German Federal Ministry of Health, February 26, 2020, youtube.com/watch?v=Fea1VY33ojE, Spahn said the following (linguistic error in the original): "That's why I'm becoming more and more convinced that the probability that this epidemic will pass Germany will not be the case."

280 Press conference by Jens Spahn at the German Federal Ministry of Health, February 27, 2020, youtube.com/watch?v=dQdQMVQuJoE

281 *Tagesschau Liveblog*, February 26, 2020, tagesschau.de/newsticker/liveblog-coronavirus-101.html

282 Press briefing RKI: "Aktuelle Informationen zu COVID-19 in Deutschland mit RKI-Präsident Lothar H. Wieler und RKI-Vizepräsident Lars Schaade" ("Current information on COVID-19 in Germany with RKI President Lothar H. Wieler and RKI Vice President Lars Schaade"), *Phoenix*, February 27, 2020, video (min. 13), youtube.com/watch?v=RNp8iwaSltc

283 RKI: "Risikobewertung zu COVID-19" ("Risk Assessment on COVID-19"), accessed February 26, 2020, web.archive.org/web/20200227151759/https://www.rki.de/DE/Content/InfAZ/N/Neuartiges_Coronavirus/Risikobewertung.html

284 "Studies on Covid-19 lethality," *Swiss Policy Research*, May 12, 2020, swprs.org/studies-on-covid-19-lethality/

285 In the same press conference, Wieler stated: "More than 80 percent of those infected develop only mild symptoms."

286 Press briefing RKI: "Aktuelle Informationen zu COVID-19 in Deutschland mit RKI-Präsident Lothar H. Wieler und RKI-Vizepräsident Lars Schaade" ("Update on COVID-19 in Germany with RKI President Lothar H. Wieler and RKI Vice President Lars Schaade"), *Phoenix*, February 27, 2020, video (min. 34), youtube.com/watch?v=RNp8iwaSltc

287 Ibid.

288 WHO: "Q&A on coronaviruses (COVID-19)," Subitem: "What are the symptoms of COVID-19?" February 23, 2020, web.archive.org/web/20200227000551/https://www.who.int/news-room/q-a-detail/q-a-coronaviruses

289 WHO: "Coronavirus disease 2019 (COVID-19) Situation Report-34," February 23, 2020.

290 "Tägliches Pressebriefing Robert-Koch-Institut zu COVID-19 in Deutschland" ("Robert Koch Institute daily press briefing on COVID-19 in Germany"), *Phoenix*, February 28, 2020, video (min. 11), youtube.com/watch?v=AsQWOAVbTNo

291 Ibid., min. 14.

292 Ibid., min. 17.

293 The 8 p.m. edition of the German news program *Tagesschau*, February 28, 2020.

294 Bill Gates: "How to respond to COVID-19," *gatesnotes.com*, February 28, 2020.

295 Bill Gates: "Responding to Covid-19—A Once-in-a-Century Pandemic?" *New England Journal of Medicine*, February 28, 2020.

296 Ibid.

297 John Ioannidis, professor of epidemiology at Stanford University, published an analysis of 23 serological studies on COVID-19 in June 2020 and determined an average (median) mortality rate of 0.26 percent. For the under-70 age group, the average mortality rate was 0.05 percent. John Ioannidis: "The infection fatality rate of Covid-19 inferred from seroprevalence data," June 8, 2020, medrxiv.org/content/10.1101/2020.05.13.20101253v2; for an overview of various studies on mortality: "Studies on Covid-19 lethality," *Swiss Policy Research*, May 12, 2020, swprs.org/studies-on-covid-19-lethali ty/

298 German Federal Ministry of Health: "Pressekonferenz zum Coronavirus" ("Press Conference on Coronavirus"), March 2, 2020, video, youtube.com/watch?v=cXBIXes4_Q4

299 Ibid., min. 10.

300 Ibid., min. 11.

301 Ibid.

302 Ibid., min. 17.

303 Ibid., min. 78.

304 Nike Heinen: "Warum dieser Mann die Epidemie kleinredet" ("Why this man talks down the epidemic"), *Welt*, March 19, 2020.

FROM TESTING MADNESS TO LOCKDOWN (MARCH 2020)

305 This question arose after reports that COVID-19 had "broken out again" in South Korea in almost 100 patients who were considered cured. RKI head Wieler explained at the RKI press briefing on April 14, 2020, that the virus might still show up in testing for a "certain time" after recovery, but only the "viral genome" and not the "reproducible virus."

306 Klaus Pfaffelmoser: "Warum die Pandemie nicht endet" ("Why the Pandemic Won't End"), *Multipolar*, May 24, 2020.

307 Ralf L. Schlenger: "PCR-Tests auf SARS-CoV-2: Ergebnisse richtig interpretieren" ("PCR testing for SARS-CoV-2: interpreting results correctly"), *Deutsches Ärzteblatt*, June 12, 2020.

308 ARD: "Nachbericht aus Berlin—Sie fragen, Bundesgesundheitsminister Spahn antwortet" ("Follow-up report from Berlin—You ask, Federal Health Minister Spahn answers"), June 14, 2020, youtube.com/watch?v=ZfWEYeokZiA; Spahn explained, "We now have to be careful that we don't have too many false positives afterwards due to extensive testing. Because the tests are not 100 percent accurate, but also have a small margin of error. And if the total number of infections continues to fall and at the same time you expand testing to millions, then you suddenly have many more false positives than actual positives. Those are the kinds of things you're confronted with down the road, and the findings."

309 Torsten Engelbrecht, Konstantin Demeter: "COVID19 PCR Tests are Scientifically Meaningless," *OffGuardian*, June 27, 2020. Excerpt: "Remarkably, in the instruction manuals of PCR tests we can also read that they are not intended as a diagnostic test, as for instance in those by Altona Diagnostics and Creative Diagnostics. To quote another one, in the product announcement of the LightMix Modular Assays produced by TIB Molbiol ... and distributed by Roche we can read: 'These assays are not intended for use as an aid in the diagnosis of coronavirus infection' and 'for research use only. Not for use in diagnostic procedures.'"

310 Robert Koch Institute: "Influenza-Wochenbericht Kalenderwoche 14/2020" ("Influenza Weekly Report Calendar Week 14/2020"), p. 4; Oliver Märtens: "Das Schweigen der Viren" ("The Silence of the Viruses"), *Multipolar*, June 21, 2020.

311 Robert Koch Institute: "Bericht zur Epidemiologie der Influenza in Deutschland, Saison 2018/19" ("Report on the epidemiology of influenza in Germany, 2018/19 season"), p. 47.

312 Robert Koch Institute: "Epidemiologisches Bulletin 16/2020" ("Epidemiological Bulletin 16/2020"), April 16, 2020, p. 3f. Excerpt: "However, many influenza cases are also associated with milder symptoms and cannot be distinguished from other colds without laboratory diagnostics, even during the influenza season."

313 Robert Koch Institute, "Täglicher Lagebericht des RKI zur Coronavirus-Krankheit-2019" ("RKI Daily Situation Report on Coronavirus Disease 2019"), July 1, 2020, p. 5.

314 "Zwei Corona-Todesfälle in Deutschland" ("Two Coronavirus Deaths in Germany"), *tagesschau.de*, March 9, 2020.

315 WHO: "WHO Director-General's opening remarks at the media briefing on COVID-19," March 11, 2020.

316 Stefan Korinth: "Schaden statt Schutz: Die familienfeindliche Corona-Politik" ("Harm instead of protection: the anti-family Coronavirus policy"), *Multipolar*, May 20, 2020.

317 Claas Relotius is a highly awarded German journalist who became especially famous when, in 2018, it was discovered that his acclaimed articles contained numerous fabrications. This was also a major scandal for the reputation of his employer, the news magazine *Der Spiegel*.

318 "Fichtner wird nicht ,Spiegel'-Chefredakteur" ("Fichtner will not become ,Spiegel' editor-in-chief"), *FAZ.net*, March 20, 2019.

319 Ullrich Fichtner: "Der Stoff, aus dem wir Menschen sind" ("The Stuff We Human Beings Are Made Of"), *Der Spiegel*, March 14, 2020.

320 Alexis Passadakis: "Austerität ist tödlich" ("Austerity is deadly"), *Freitag*, March 18, 2020. Excerpt: "The crisis of the health care system in Italy is a consequence of the bank bailout after the financial crisis. The fact that hospitals were sacrificed for this is now becoming a danger"; Mélissa Godin: "Why Is Italy's Coronavirus Outbreak So Bad?" *Time*, March 10, 2020. Excerpt: "'The continuous cuts—to care and to research—are obviously a problem right now,' Lorenzo Casani, the health director of a clinic for elderly people in Lombardy says. 'We were not prepared. We do not have enough doctors for the people.'"

321 "Deutschland hat viermal so viele Intensivbetten wie Italien" ("Germany has four times as many intensive care beds as Italy"), *FAZ.net*, April 2, 2020.

322 Simona Ravizza: "Milano, terapie intensive al collasso per l'influenza: già 48 malati gravi molte operazioni rinviate" ("Milan, intensive care units collapse during the flu: already 48 seriously ill, many operations postponed"), *Corriere della Sera*, January 10, 2018.

323 Matthias Rüb: "Warum sterben in Italien so viele?" ("Why are so many dying in Italy?"), *FAZ.net*, March 20, 2020.

324 Sarah Newey: "Why have so many coronavirus patients died in Italy?" *The Telegraph*, March 23, 2020.

325 Robert Koch Institute/Federal Statistical Office: "Sterblichkeit, Todesursachen und regionale Unterschiede" ("Mortality, Causes of Death, and Regional Differences"), Gesundheitsberichterstattung des Bundes (Federal Health Reports), Issue 52, April 2011, p. 27. Excerpt: "In the confidential part of the death certificate—in accordance with the WHO international form for the certification of causes of death—a causal chain should be presented, if possible, from the underlying condition that was decisive for the death leading to the immediate cause of death. However, only the underlying condition coded in the state offices is then included in the statistics as the cause of death."

326 Marcus Klöckner: "Die Corona-Toten: eine Medienzahl" ("The Coronavirus Dead: A Media Count"), *Multipolar*, April 13, 2020.

327 Florian Rötzer: "Feinstaubpartikel als Viren-Vehikel" ("Fine Particles as Viral Vehicles"), *Telepolis*, March 21, 2020.

328 Leonardo Setti et al.: "Relazione circa l'effetto dell'inquinamento da particolato atmosferico e la diffusione di virus nella popolazione" ("Report on the effect of particulate air pollution and the spread of viruses in the population"), University of Bologna, March 2020.

329 Amanda MacMillan, "Hospitals Overwhelmed by Flu Patients Are Treating Them in Tents," *Time*, January 18, 2018.

330 The medical director of an ambulance service in Rhineland-Palatinate wrote in a call for help to the Federal Ministry of the Interior (the letter is in the author's possession) of a "capacity emergency and mass influx of sick people" with "disaster-equivalent effects" due to the flu epidemic. The situation had repeatedly been "unmanageable" in March 2018.

331 The 8 p.m. edition of the German news program *Tagesschau*, March 20, 2020.

332 Paul Schreyer: "Coronavirus: Irreführung bei den Fallzahlen nun belegt" ("Coronavirus: Misleading Case Numbers Now Proven"), *Multipolar*, March 28, 2020. The article also appeared as a podcast and was viewed more than 300,000 times before being temporarily deleted by YouTube. The mainstream media largely ignored the connections; the *Multipolar* article led to a single (!) follow-up report in the mainstream media, an article in the Münchner Merkur: "Coronavirus-Zahlen in Deutschland steigen rasant: Verzerrt eine wenig beachtete Zahl die Statistik?" ("Coronavirus numbers in Germany soar: Is a little-noticed figure distorting the statistics?"), *Merkur.de*, April 1, 2020.

333 "Keine Empfehlungen, sondern Regeln" ("No recommendations, just rules"), *tagesschau.de*, March 22, 2020; "Coronavirus: Merkel zu neuen Regeln—Maximal zwei Personen erlaubt" ("Coronavirus: Merkel on new rules—Maximum two people allowed"), youtube.com/watch?v=6pQgZLg0xog

EPILOGUE: ABOUT DEATH—AND ERROR

334 "For Every Child, Every Right: The Convention on the Rights of the Child at a crossroads," UNICEF, November 2019, p. 2; "Jeden Tag sterben 15 000 Kinder" ("Every day, 15,000 children die"), *Die Zeit Online*, October 19, 2017.

335 *ZDF Markus Lanz*, broadcast of April 21, 2020, video (min. 68).

336 Message from the Robert Koch Institute on its own Twitter account, July 6, 2020.